Playing with Purpose

SH
For Lisa and for Charlie and Eliza:
True inspirations of creativity and curiosity.

HL
For Thomas, Katherine and Peter:
My reminders of what, and who, is important.

Playing with Purpose

How Experiential Learning
Can Be More Than a Game

STEVE HUTCHINSON

HELEN LAWRENCE

GOWER

Published by
Gower Publishing Limited
Wey Court East
Union Road
Farnham
Surrey
GU9 7PT
England

Gower Publishing Company
Suite 420
101 Cherry Street
Burlington
VT 05401-4405
USA

www.gowerpublishing.com

Steve Hutchinson and Helen Lawrence have asserted their moral right under the Copyright, Designs and Patents Act, 1988, to be identified as the authors of this work.

British Library Cataloguing in Publication Data
Hutchinson, Steve.
  Playing with purpose : how experiential learning can be
  more than a game.
  1. Experiential learning. 2. Active learning.
  3. Employees--Training of--Methodology.
  I. Title II. Lawrence, Helen.
  153.1'52-dc22

Library of Congress Cataloging-in-Publication Data

Library of Congress Control Number: 2011924186

ISBN   978-1-4094-0805-5 (pbk)
ISBN   978-1-4094-0806-2 (ebk)

MIX
Paper from
responsible sources
FSC
www.fsc.org   FSC® C018575

Printed and bound in Great Britain by the
MPG Books Group, UK

Contents

List of Figures

The only source of knowledge is experience
Albert Einstein

About the Authors

After completing his PhD in Behavioural Ecology and working in academia, Dr Steve Hutchinson led development programmes at the Universities of York and Leeds. He now owns and runs his own development consultancy and has designed and led acclaimed courses and events for a huge range of organizations and institutions, both in the UK and abroad. A highly skilled facilitator and trainer, he is both a Vitae GRADschool national course director and a programme director for the Leadership Foundation for Higher Education. He is a qualified trainer, coach and practitioner of Neuro-Linguistic Programming. He writes articles and chapters on a range of topics from creativity to leadership and motivation. *Playing with Purpose* is his second book.

Dr Helen Lawrence completed a PhD in Sociolinguistic Variation and worked in the academic sector for a number of years, publishing, teaching and lecturing. Discovering a passion for helping people realize their potential she moved into the field of training and development. For five years she worked at the University of York, taking a lead role in developing and delivering training programmes for staff and students. In 2008 she set up her own training and development business, and works with individuals, teams and institutions in the research, educational and not-for-profit sectors. Helen is also a local and national Vitae GRADschool tutor; an accredited Myers Briggs Type Indicator practitioner; and a trained Coactive Coach.

Acknowledgements

If I see a little further it is because I have stood on the shoulders of giants.
Attributed to a variety of sources including
Bernard of Chartres and Sir Isaac Newton

For the ideas, ethos and styles within this book, professionally we both owe a great deal to similar sources, including, but not limited to:

The directors and tutors of the Vitae/UK GRAD organization, Heather Sears, Jamie McDonald, Odette Dewhurst, Heather Stout, Paul Toombs, Tim Bentham, Dave Filipović-Carter, Sara Shinton, Fiona Denney, Caron King and the good people in Human Resources at the Universities of York and Leeds, and anyone who's ever collected a milk-bottle top for us. Special thanks to Mike Rawlins.

Note to the Reader

Training and facilitation is often a very personal experience, with you and the learning group cosseted out of sight of prying eyes. However, this book was a joint venture and the concepts and philosophies presented herein are shared or collective. As such we've shamelessly alternated between the use of 'I' and 'we'. So, to help the reader, the use of 'I' is often found in the solo anecdotes and 'we' binds the more abstract material.

Preface: Why Read this Book and How to Use It

In every real man a child is hidden that wants to play.

Friedrich Nietzsche (Philosopher)

Some time ago I was on a departmental 'away day'. There had been a number of presentations about our organization's strategic vision for the future and there had been a similar number of dry SWOT (strengths, weaknesses, opportunities, threats) discussions about how our department would react to the vision. Collectively we were then tasked with forming team reactions and action plans for the future and asked to prepare a presentation for the rest of the department. Our team kicked about a number of ideas and we were in the process of putting together a standard flipchart-led presentation of all the extra activity and work that we were going to undertake. At this point, someone decided that having an away day to land ourselves with more work was pointless, and what we really needed to do was simplify.

Inspired by the SWOT analysis, we decided that we'd been buzzing round like flies for too long and we were in danger of being 'swatted'. So we took the insect metaphor and developed it into how we as a team should be more like bees and less like flies. We put together five key principles (which even now I can restate) and instead of a presentation we prepared a skit which involved the whole team hovering round like bees with paper cups on our noses, and acting out the five new strategies.

Come presentation time, the other groups gave many bullet points and we had a natural history documentary with everyone from team leader to office administrator involved. Needless to say this was probably viewed in less-than-ideal terms by our boss. However, months and years later, everyone present could still restate the key apian principles and still talked about that part of the day. The challenging of process had had a profound effect on the team involved, and the fun experience had changed the way the team engaged.

All it took was paper cups and courage to challenge the process.

This book is written with that spirit, and asks how can you as a trainer, manager, people developer or coach get powerful lessons from the simplest of objects and situations? We hope that it will act as an inspiration for anyone interested in people development and is prepared to risk livening up office meetings or encourage people to talk and honestly engage with each other.

Over the past decade, both of us have spent a great deal of our professional lives playing games. As professional trainers and developers we've had groups building towers, rolling balls, blowing whistles and balancing buckets to supposedly illustrate and teach vital 'real-life' principles and concepts. What became clear to us both is that most human resource departments or staff development sections have a training cupboard full of this type of store-bought experiences. And, despite the sometimes massive financial outlay for these toys, they are in the minds of the learners involved, often little more than games. They roll balls, balance buckets and learn something about teamwork and tolerance. Then the training day ends and they go back to business as usual.

We believe that real learning can only be said to have taken place when, back in 'the office', something changes as a result of the intervention. Balls, buckets and ropes can provide a new experience; but only if that experience is mined for the full impact (physical, mental or emotional) will learning take place and change occur. This book is about how you as a facilitator, coach, manager or trainer can invent or reinvigorate an artificial learning experience and have it be more than a game. Or, in the form of a short question:

Is it possible to facilitate and extract real learning from artificial situations?

We believe that the answer to this question is, of course, 'yes'; but it leads to three others:

- How can you do this more effectively?
- How can you create new games/studies/scenarios that can access the kind of learning you're interested in?
- How can you reinvigorate old games to facilitate real learning?

We hope this book provides some answers to these questions.

The book is constructed in three main sections:

Part I provides an examination of the concepts and skills required by the creator and facilitator of experiential learning opportunities. This section deals with how to take an idea into an exercise or an experience that will be effective in the training room.

Part II offers an overview of the skills and techniques associated with helping participants to extract, translate and transform any training-room learning back into day-to-day reality.

Part III presents a series of eight development issues; each presented in a separate chapter with our approach to the issue and suggested activities suitable to that scenario.

This is not a book about 'how to be a trainer' – we assume that you have some experience in doing this already. As such we don't cover furniture layout, welcoming participants, having breaks, PowerPoint-craft, storytelling or any of the other facets of being a professional developer.[1]

It is our hope that you will find the suggested ideas and activities useful. Sometimes we've presented fully working ideas – please feel free to use them exactly as they are presented. Sometimes we've presented partially formed ideas and possibilities, our intention being that if we can inspire you to do it for yourself this is a far more valuable

---

1   If you need a great overview of professional training practice, we'd recommend *How to Run a Great Workshop* by Nikki Highmore Sims (2006).

resource. Hopefully, by seeing our approach to the dilemmas explicitly laid out, you'll feel confident to develop your own solutions. Finally, we are aware that many of the ideas presented here are based on activities that have passed into the 'received wisdom' of the training and development field. Where we are able we will acknowledge the authors or creators of these; please forgive us if we have missed references and do contact us if you can fill any of the gaps.

SJH and HRL 2011

The Concept of Experiential Learning

1 *Optimizing Artificial Experiential Learning*

Pleasure is the flower that passes, remembrance the lasting perfume.
Jean de Boufflers (French Statesman and Writer)

Learning is grounded in experience. As trainers and facilitators, then, we must seek to create experiences from which people can learn. Challenge, success, failure, conflict and harmony can all provide powerful opportunities for experiential learning.

We believe that it is essential, in this creative process, to strike a balance between challenging realism and memorable stimulation or fun. Unless both components are addressed, it is unlikely that any real benefit will be gained from any intervention. In addition, unless any learning is reviewed and fully discussed, realized and deconstructed, much of the value of the experience may still be lost. As such, any experience does not need to be expensive to be powerful and in fact often the reverse is true.

Training and Human Resouces (HR) departments are bombarded with advertisements for a wide array of the different kits, registered techniques and materials available. It is easy to become dazzled by beautiful packaging and shining testimonials about the value of professionally produced resources, and for the primary purpose of the intervention to become lost. More significantly, training resources which are purchased 'off the shelf' will by their very nature not fit the learning needs of a specific group or individual so well as a tailored activity created for the purpose.

In short, the primary aim of any teaching or training intervention must be for the participants to learn and not to simply have an experience, however glossy.

Yet in our field, many professional educators seem to have lost sight of this core truth. For instance, do you as a teacher, trainer or manager start a session with an 'energizer' because your colleagues all do, or because you want your participants to enjoy a fun activity; or is it because you need your participants to be thinking clearly?

Focusing on the learning first, instead of the beautifully wrapped training game, gives far greater sustainable return:

- Educational sustainability – with lessons that last long after the intervention has ended.
- Financial sustainability – all the new learning activities suggested herein are commonplace and cheap/free, and the questions and insights here can breathe new life into activities already in your store cupboard.
- Creative sustainability – by focusing on the learning possibilities that objects offer you'll avoid staleness as a teacher or trainer, as there are *always* new objects around.

If we could first know where we are, and whither we are tending, we could then better judge what to do, and how to do it.

Abraham Lincoln (US President)

Why Play Games?

Activities and games are used in training and development settings because human beings learn from experience. Introducing an activity into a training session guarantees that each individual experiences the same event, so the learning which can be extracted in the group has a common point of reference. It is also quicker, cheaper and more convenient than using real-life experiences as source material. Therein, however, is both the activity's blessing and its curse, because for all the advantages it provides, in the eyes of the participants it isn't real. The skill of the facilitator here is in extracting real learning from artificial situations.

It's important to keep the perceived *unreality* of the experience at the front of your mind when designing and offering the activity to a training room (as this can help you to overcome potential pitfalls and challenges from groups), but it's also vital to keep in mind the reality of the exercise (after all it was real, insofar as it actually happened) in the review and learning extraction.

While we were writing one of the full-formed exercises that appear in this book, I mentioned to a colleague of ours (whom we rate and respect as a trainer) that we had written a brand new exercise. Her response surprised me: 'Wow. I wouldn't have the first idea where to start with something like that.' But there is no mystery, no magic that needs to be woven in to the fabric of a powerful learning tool. Rather, at the foundation of every new activity, there needs to be a clear understanding of what the learning point is. The key to success of any activity or scenario is this:

First, focus on the learning.

If the learning intentions and outcomes are foremost in your mind right from the start then the chances of success are far higher. Get it the wrong way round (game first, learning second), and you run a very real risk of creating a pointless distraction.

Probably the best way to explain how this process works in practice is to describe our creative process in the design of a new activity. Generally, when we take an inventory of our training creations, we've taken the following steps:

- inspiration;
- realism based on experience;
- theoretical understanding and criticism;
- testing and piloting;
- adaptation and reconsiderations.

These steps feed into one another and can be visually represented in Figure 1.1 opposite.

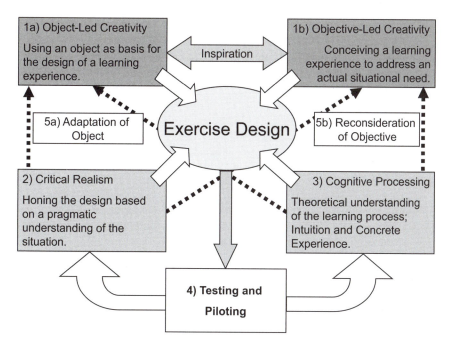

Figure 1.1   Overarching experimental exercise design process

Sources of Inspiration

Inspiration for us comes from two main places: 1) having a clear idea of a desired outcome and asking 'How could that be achieved?' and then being on the lookout for kit that would be useful in achieving that outcome; and 2) seeing something, anything, and asking 'How could that be used?'

Practitioner's Exercise

Take a blank sheet of paper and a pen. Your objective is to enable a group to explore issues around *customer service*. List ten different training possibilities or activities that you could run with each of the following resources:

A teapot

Toilet paper

Paperclips

Don't reject any of your ideas out of hand. Everything around you has some sort of learning potential. Apply the words attributed to Charlemagne,* 'Let my armies be the rocks and the trees and the birds in the sky.'

Note: * In the film *Indiana Jones and the Last Crusade,* Henry Jones attributes these words to the Roman emperor, though we can find no evidence that Charlemagne actually said it.

Practitioner's Exercise

Listing 20 for each, consider what learning outcomes of *any type* might be served by using the following objects:

Leaves

Ten mobile phones

A pair of socks

By focusing on quantity you will find yourself less concerned about the quality of the ideas you are generating – thus allowing your creativity free rein to think of possibilities rather than restricting yourself to the uses expected of an item or the typical way of meeting learning objectives.

Object-Led Creativity (1a)

In order to use objects as inspiration it is useful to notice possibilities in all manner of different contexts, and then become a collector of oddments. In order to illustrate this point, we went through the training bags that we carry *every day* to find out what we both saw as *essential* kit. This is what we found:

Elastic Bands	Post it® notes	Treasury tags
Sticky labels	A selection of 10–15 mixed holiday postcards	Balloons
Coloured pens	Drinking straws	Standard playing cards
Paper clips	Marbles	Tennis balls
Red, green and blue plastic milk bottle tops	Dice	String or wool
BluTac®	Masking tape	A blindfold (or square of cloth suitable for same purpose)

In addition, the following can usually be found in any office, seminar room or training venue:

Office paper (A4)	Wooden or plastic drinks stirrers	Sweets
Drinking cups	Paper plates	Spoons
Toilet roll/paper napkins	Flipchart paper and pens	Old newspapers or magazines

Having a reserve of interesting objects at your disposal offers constant possibilities and keeps your creative juices flowing. In addition to this, learners can often find their mental faculties are stimulated by their tactile senses. I ran a team review recently where a quiet and reserved team came almost immediately to life when asked to explain their departmental dynamics and given a box of sweets with which to do it.

Practitioner's Exercise

Take an object, any object, from within arm's reach. Pick it up and, perhaps for the first time, really notice it properly. Now consider the following:

Use your Senses

What colour is the article you're noticing? What size, weight, texture? What might these properties provide or represent in a learning situation?

Be Metaphorical

Could your pen represent a person? Could your ruler be a bridge? Could your desktop mouse-mat be a map? Can a paper cup be representative of a department in your organization?

Incidentally, a twist on this is to take a large number of different objects or pictures into a room and ask participants to choose the one that best represents something else (for example, how they feel about their team, how their boss operates or how their career is working out so far). You'll be amazed by the insight that they give when an innocent object becomes a conduit for what they already know, but can't or won't articulate.

Scale Up or Scale Down

Is something possible with many of the same article that might not be with one? What about isolating one paperclip from your stationery pot?

Distinctiveness

Is the article particularly unusual in some way?

Current Use and Purpose

What do you know of that article? How might this link with activity? For example a drinking straw is long, rigid, flexible, hollow, coloured and light. What might these characteristics allow you to do? What would it be totally ill suited for? Could asking a learner to carry out a task with an object completely unfit for purpose pique their creativity?

For instance, in one minute, this is what we came up with for *training possibilities with drinking straws*:

• plumbing pipework (to transport water/air/sound);

• building rods;

- multiple straws could represent multiple people;

- representation of flexibility or rigidity of role;

- pipette;

- loadbearing (for rafts or bridge-type builds);

- resources (use them as currency in a trade game);

- use for spelling letters;

- blowpipes;

- cut to different lengths (for drawing lots);

- stuck down as a collage;

- stems of artificially create foliage.

For any given learning outcome, most of these ideas probably would be rejected at some stage in the design process. However, all of them offer *something* if you're thinking creatively.

This consideration of random objects as tools to facilitate learning soon takes on a life of its own and you'll find yourself becoming more lateral, creative and flexible in your trainings and in other areas of your life and work. If you feel your creativity needs a tune-up, Edward de Bono's classic *Lateral Thinking* (1990) offers a great place to start. A further bonus of your new creative approach is that you can start to reinterpret old shop-bought existing activities for new audiences and objectives and in ways that aren't obvious if you stick to the given instructions.

Objective-Driven Inspiration (1b)

As we mentioned at the opening of this chapter, alongside the object-driven inspiration it is absolutely vital to consider the *point* of the interaction. Without such consideration even the most beautiful, tactile and well-conceived exercise is no more than a game. These considerations could include those listed below.

Practitioner's Enquiries

What is the underlying issue, problem or situation that this exercise will address?

What need *must* I meet? What is essential, and what is desirable?

Is there one desired outcome or several?

What would success be? What are the lessons I want these people to learn?

How do I want the people to interact with the materials?

How do I want them to ideally engage with each other?

What will allow these people to embed the learning?

What would I, personally, like to get out of this session?

If the session were perfect, what would change as a result of it?

How specific are your objectives and outcomes? Are they clear, or do they need refining?

What scenarios, situations, case studies or simulations have I already seen that I could tweak to meet these differing objectives?

Critical Realism (2)

Having enthusiastically created and developed new ideas, it is of course essential to integrate a reality check into your design process. You may have a fabulous idea for an exercise using planks and ropes, but if your training room provides insufficient space then all the learning potential of your activity will evaporate. A dose of critical realism here is essential and the following questions provide a framework for this:

Practitioner's Enquiries

Are there restrictions I need to consider? (For example, time/space)

How flexible is the space? How elastic is the time allocation?

How many people is this exercise for?

What might go wrong? Do I have a contingency plan?

How could a difficult participant sabotage this? (Through both their words and behaviour.)

How long will this take a) to do, and b) to review properly? (See Part II, pages 27–44 of this book regarding unpacking and reviewing the learning.)

How portable is the activity and equipment?

What is required from me as an instructor? Would I need an assistant?

How established are the group and does this matter in relation to this exercise?

What am I going to be doing while the people are busy? How will this impact my ability to fully notice what is happening and so lead a review?

Is this activity suitable for anyone or does it discriminate? (See Chapter 10 – Exploring Diversity Issues.)

What instructions do I need to prepare?

At these initial stages, regardless of objective or object-led inspiration, it is important not to reject an idea too quickly. Even a seemingly 'poor' idea can often be adapted to function perfectly well. We find it useful to ask the question:

How could we make this better?

rather than 'What's wrong with this idea?', thus placing our focus positively and productively.

Design and Cognitive Processing (3)

I hear and I forget. I see and I remember. I do and I understand.

Confucius (Philosopher)

In order to create a learning experience that has real impact, you need to know *why* you want the impact in the first place and what sort of intellectual or theoretical knowledge you need the learners to gain. As such you'll need to know some of the theory behind the objective of the exercise (that is, to make an activity suited to leadership outcomes you need an understanding of some of the current leadership theories). This is necessary in part to run an effective review and in part to satisfy the needs of the learners who may need a theoretical foundation to help embed the experience.

THEORETICAL KNOWLEDGE AND UNDERSTANDING OF THE EXPERIENTIAL LEARNING PROCESS (3a)

There is a wealth of theoretical information available and the aim here is to replicate as little of it as possible. However, it is necessary to have a general understanding of experiential learning theory and a working knowledge of the differing learning styles that people have, in order to create a fully rounded and comprehensive learning experience. We find that David Kolb's *Experiential Learning Theory* (1984) is essential to underpin the design of our learning activities.

Over many years research (best captured in the book *Experiential Learning: Experience as the Source of Learning and Development* (1984), David Kolb set out a seminal learning styles model which is widely recognized by practitioners as being a key tool to help understand practical learning.

Kolb's work clarifies four distinct learning areas, based on a four-fold cycle of learning (see Figure 1.2). In lay-speak, these four areas could be classed as 'do and feel', 'watch and review', 'theorize and think' and 'plan and do' (or 'experimenting' leading back into 'do and feel'). In Kolb's terms, an 'immediate or concrete experience' gives foundations for 'observations and reflections'. These are processed and filtered into abstract concepts giving rise to an understanding that can be actively tested in new experiences.

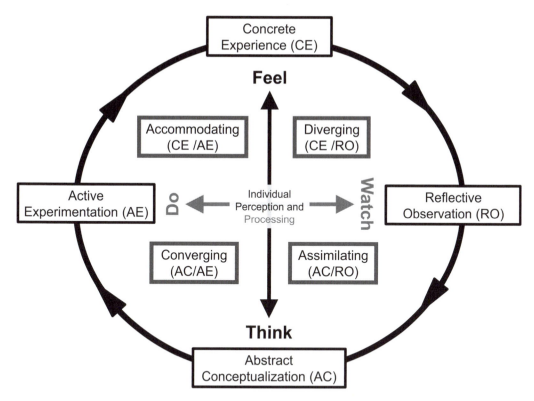

Figure 1.2   The experiential learning cycle (adapted from Kolb)

Kolb's work is clearly far more complex than this, but this core essence seems to contain the key information that a training practitioner needs to know. Kolb says that ideally (and so by omission, not every time) the learning process needs to visit each step of the cycle. It is thus vital that a learning activity contains space and opportunity for participants to be in each place.

Kolb provides an explanation that each individual will have a unique learning style, developed from birth, through adolescence, to specialized adulthood; and shaped by communal, organizational and educational experience. Our individual learning styles are affected by choices that we make, which are represented here as two continua ('perception' and 'processing') with conflicting modes at either end: 'feeling' versus 'thinking', and 'doing' versus 'watching'.

Kolb proposed that an individual cannot simultaneously do both ('think' *and* 'feel', or 'do' *and* 'watch') but the *urge* to do both creates conflict. This conflict is resolved through the choices we make as individuals when confronted with a new learning circumstance. We internally decide whether we wish to do *or* watch, and at the same time we decide whether to think *or* feel. The result of these choices, Kolb said, produces a preferred learning style.

An individual primarily will choose a way of grasping the experience (either to watch or to do), and then choose a way to transform it into something real and useable (either by thinking or feeling).

Practitioner's Enquiries

How could you manipulate the opportunities for these types of decisions in your exercise design?

Could you enforce an initial period of planning and no action?

Could you insist on a quick and early sub-deadline to prevent any extended planning?

What effect would these manipulations have on the individuals' and groups' engagement? How would it affect any learning opportunities?

Could you 'fishbowl' an activity, so one group/individual can learn by observation from the mistakes of another?*

Could you provide a great deal of structure to an activity, providing a long list of rules and necessary back-story, or would it be better to leave the objectives vague and nebulous?

Could you use familiar theories or practices to help a group think through a new type of task?

Could you arrange it so that a group were deprived of prior theoretical knowledge and had to feel their way through an exercise?

Note: * See Chapter 5 for a full description of this technique.

Learners will opt to either observe or reflect on what happens in an exercise or just to jump in and play around. In addition, they will choose to translate the meaning by either thinking in an abstract sense or by using their senses and feelings of the reality.

Building on to this simple core, Kolb's work also contains a four-way definition of personal learning styles (each comprising of a combination of two individual choices) for which he uses the terms: 'diverging'; 'assimilating'; 'converging'; and 'accommodating'.

As with the translation of any theory to actual human beings, the next level should be taken more as guidance than gospel. Most people exhibit obvious preferences for a certain learning style and these do not change a great deal from situation to situation. So it is worth considering the characteristics typical to a generic individual with a preferred learning style. This overview of the topic is adapted from *A Handbook of Teaching and Learning in Higher Education – Enhancing Academic Practice* by Heather Fry, Steve Ketteridge and Stephanie Marshall (1999), which also provides much food for thought in other areas.

Diverging

Kolb called this style 'diverging' because people with a preference in this area tend to excel in situations that require divergent processing, such as idea generation and creative thinking. Generally, people with the diverging style prefer to work in groups. They tend to listen well and respond to personal feedback.

Assimilating

An 'assimilating' learning preference is for a concise, logical approach where ideas and concepts take precedence over people. Generally, individuals with this style value time to think things through rationally and analytically. Learning experiences that are not clearly structured are often more challenging to an individual with an assimilating preference.

Converging

People with a preference for a 'converging' style like to experiment with new ideas, to simulate and to work with practical applications. They tend to be drawn to technical tasks, and are often less concerned with people and interpersonal aspects of tasks.

Accommodating

Individuals with an 'accommodating' preference commonly act on 'gut instinct' rather than logical analysis, and prefer a practical trial-and-error approach. As such, huge quantities of written rules and task information may frustrate them. They may tend to rely on others for information than carry out their own analysis.

Practitioner's Enquiries

Do the activities you design typically cater to a certain learning style over others?

Is *your* personal learning style obvious from the way you tackle exercise design?

Do your games include a mixture of 'task' and 'people'; 'divergent' (what could we do?) and 'convergent' (what will we do and by when?) processing; theoretical and practical, or is it better to deliberately limit the types of experience that an exercise will provide?

How could you encourage (or coerce/rule) individuals or groups to experience different types of learning to their comfortable norms?

Will your task need *all* of a group to cooperate in order to succeed (whatever 'success' means in this context), or is it possible for one or two group members to (for example) solve the puzzle without the input of the rest of the group?

PRACTICAL LEARNING STYLES

Often the work of David Kolb is known to people through the model of Peter Honey and Alan Mumford (1982), who worked on learning styles from an industrial and management perspective. To describe the steps of the learning cycle they use the terms 'activist', 'reflector', 'theorist' and 'pragmatist'. For more information on this, see Honey and Mumford's work from the early 1980s (referenced at the end of this book). Their model does not quite overlay Kolb's, but has clear similarities and provides a helpful shortcut to enable groups to quickly understand, for example, the theory behind the review of an activity.

Honey and Mumford's Learning Style	Roughly equates to Kolb's Learning Style	In a Nutshell	Broad Descriptor
Activist	Accommodating	'Get stuck in'	They seek (team) challenge and thrive on immediate experience, open-minded but bored with repetition and extended implementation.
Reflector	Diverging	'Stand well back'	They gather data, ponder and analyze, delay reaching conclusions, and listen thoughtfully before speaking.
Theorist	Assimilating	'Think it through'	They process in logical steps, assimilate data into cogent theories. Rational and objective.
Pragmatist	Converging	'Plan practically'	They relish problem-solving and quick decision-making. Practical and innovative they tend to be bored with long discussions.

Practitioner's Enquiries

Do your exercises provide scope for learners to do some or all of the above?

How will different individuals react to the task you set them? How might the differences here strengthen the learning experience?

Note: We firmly believe that 'liking' or 'disliking' an exercise on the part of a learner has very little to do with the learning inherent in it. Of course you'll want to design supportive and positively challenging exercises and experiences, but don't be tempted to confuse *liking* with *learning* on the part of the participant.

AN ADDITIONAL LAYER OF VARIETY

In addition to the various learning styles and models already discussed, it is also worth considering the modality of processing that an individual learner will prefer. A helpful simplification here is to consider whether an individual has a preferred 'visual', 'auditory', 'kinaesthetic' or 'textual'[1] learning modality.

---

1   For more information here you may wish to consult VARK learning styles material, (http://www.vark-learn.com) where VARK stands for the Visual, Aural, Read/write, and Kinesthetic sensory means that are used for learning. Alternatively a brief understanding of Neurolinguistic Programming theory (try Knight (1995) as a useful guide) will give similar insight.

Visual

Learners with a visual preference use and value the depiction of information in maps, charts, graphs, labelled diagrams and other symbols that are used to represent what could have been presented in words.

Aural/Auditory

Learners with a preference for auditory information value content that is spoken or heard. Often people with this preferred modality want to talk in order to think, not to think first and then talk. Group discussions and aural briefings are ideal for aural processors.

Kinaesthetic

People who prefer this mode of learning are often the hands-on doers who thrive on the reality of case studies, games, practices and applications. As such it is important to remember that there will be certain advantages (at least in terms of familiarity) for them in any sort of experiential learning situation.

Textual

Learners with a textual modality preference value information displayed as words – both input and output. Often, when we write a new activity the concept is very simple, but we surround it by (often extraneous) written material. This is partly to represent the reality of most work-based situations, but partly to stimulate the theoretically-driven and textual learners.

Practitioner's Enquiries

For any given exercise how are you providing 'input' of information to the participants? Textually, graphically or audibly? What outputs do you require from any given task? How do these suit different learning modalities? (For example, asking for a skit or news-anchor style presentation of the captured learning will appeal to a very different sort of learner to a text-based report, or group discussion.)

Does your designed experience consider a balance of learning modalities, or does it heavily favour one? Balance or imbalance is neither good nor bad – just different. Success in design is that any difference has been considered rather than being accidental.

LEARNING STYLES AND MODALITIES – THE BOTTOM LINE

In any given group, team, collective or even individual there will be an unknown (initially to you and, almost certainly, to them) distribution of learning preferences, styles, modalities and types. It is vital that any exercise or experience that you design is built on a clear understanding that people learn in different ways. Care is needed to ensure that even a well-executed design is not wasted because it suits only those individuals who happen to learn in the same way as you! If it is possible to work out the designer's preferred learning style, modality or type from an exercise, the design could probably be considerably improved by the application of fresh eyes with a different personal style.

Returning to the overarching schematic of exercise design (from page 5), we now arrive at Experience and Intuition.

Concrete Experience and Intuition (3b)

As your expertise builds, you'll start to instinctively sense what will 'work' in an exercise and what won't. In order to help you to gauge this, it is worth keeping a log of information to help the redesign process or to create new materials.

LEARNING FROM YOUR EXPERIENCES OF GROUPS' EXPERIENCES…

In order to catalogue your trialled materials and improve and build upon them, the types of information that you may want to be keeping records of are:

Practitioner's Questions

How long did that activity actually take? Did it need more or less time than you'd planned?

What surprised you? What unforeseen issues did the activity reveal?

What went well/badly?

What would you change and what might the impact of that be?

Where were the points where an activity might have taken a whole new direction?

Were there lines of activity or approach that were taken that surprised you? Did you see new possibilities that the groups missed?

Were there *accidental* ambiguities in any rules or briefing materials?

What formal feedback did any activity solicit from the people involved?

Note: Beware of taking feedback from participants at face value. Sometimes a negative comment can be indicative of a participant who has been stretched intellectually and has found the experience uncomfortable. Such discomfort may be indicative of learning. Or it could indicate that an individual has moved from being intellectually or emotionally stretched into mentally shutting down. Of course, repeated similar negative feedback is a clear sign that the activity needs to be revised.

It is often these insights that give the activity far more impact. For instance, we once wrote an activity with a very simple set of rules. So simple in fact that some learning groups decided to start breaking them. Instead of revising the activity, however, we allowed this to open up discussions of 'values' (that is, why were some rules breakable and some sacrosanct) which made the long-term value of the simple exercise increase dramatically.

Alongside this personal experience, there is a great deal of wisdom to be gained by learning vicariously. Watching other people running exercises and case studies, talking to other trainers and managers and listening to coffee-break conversations about what the participants *really* thought are all helpful ways of building your expertise.

TRUST YOUR GUT – HOW INTUITION CAN HELP

Intuition comes from a variety of sources: empathy with the participants; experience of other situations; the 'big picture' which comes from the wealth of small details that you have in your mind as you consider a possible activity. Warning bells can ring as you consider a possibility which seems feasible – never ignore these, but revisit the critical realism section (above) to pinpoint why specifically the bell is ringing. Similarly, you may sense that a rather ordinary idea will have sparkle when tried out in a learning environment. It may be that you have picked up a facet of an activity that you struggle to articulate at first. If in doubt, go with your gut feeling and ask other people for comments before piloting the idea.

For example, I once watched a very common, simple and well-tested exercise die in the hands of an in-house trainer. The participants (a fairly senior management team) were required to roll small balls down tracks in order to build collaboration, planning and teamwork. This had 'worked' as an exercise many times in the past, but on a whim the trainer decided to move the group from the hidden safety of the training room to a very public grassy space right outside the main administrative centre of the organization. My guts told me that this was probably a mistake, but I held my tongue in case the trainer had consciously chosen to put the group under observation and stress. The team, that had been functional and bonded, promptly fell to pieces because their juniors, seniors and management colleagues came and watched from their various windows. The group decided not to engage with the task for fear of looking foolish, and rather than review with them around this discomfort, the trainer took them back inside for another 'game'. My senses, intuition and experience had combined here to tell me that the environment was wrong for an otherwise solid exercise. Yet even in this case, some good learning could have been extracted with a well-run task review. (For more on reviewing a task, see Chapter 2 'Extracting the Lesson: How to Review, Capture and Amplify the Learning'.)

The more you notice your 'sense' of an activity in the design phase the more you will be prepared for potential problems and conversely the fewer ideas you'll reject out of hand.

Returning to our conceptual schematic of design above, once you have the inspiration, theoretical underpinning, experience and intuition, you can now try running the exercise. Each main chapter of the book deals with a certain type of reason for learning, and so here is probably a good place to bookmark, and then revisit when you've read the main chapters that are of interest to you. Then come back to this place and pick up the fine-tuning process once more.

Practitioner's Enquiries

What do your guts and intuition tell you about how your exercise might work?

What would be the worst that could happen? (How could you pre-empt and mitigate against these risks?)

How could you sabotage your own activity?

How could you extract learning from any eventuality?

What will you do if the team don't understand the brief?

What will you do if they solve or complete the exercise in a quarter of the time allocated?

If you want to continue here, let's assume for a moment that you have a prototype idea. It's now time to test and review it before it goes live.

Testing and Piloting (4)

Fall seven times, stand up eight.
Japanese Proverb

An idea will only ever be a possibility until you try it out. Our advice is to pilot a new activity with a critical but friendly group, one you can be fairly sure won't deliberately sabotage the activity and will provide useful feedback. In some ways the advice to pilot a new endeavour before it counts seems like common sense. However, when the raw materials are 'amateur' it is vital that the learning outcomes and mechanisms are *better* than if the kit is completely 'professional' and polished.

Sample Practitioner's Questions for Test Groups

Was it clear what you were supposed to be doing?

Was it clear why you were supposed to be doing it?

At which point was the information unclear?

Did you feel that you needed more time on any given part?

Did you notice any errors?

What did you like? Dislike?

What do you think the point of the exercise is?

After the test run, rather than ask a group 'What do you think?', you may get more helpful feedback with some more targeted questioning. Remember that a group's feedback is just feedback – not absolute truth. For instance, if they say the brief was 'unclear' that could be a good thing, providing that the brief was written with ambiguity in mind.

Trust your intuition again, make the necessary changes and re-pilot. We both find that dinner parties and family gatherings are good for this sort of test-flight. The evenings just fly by…

SETTING AN EXERCISE UP IN THE *RIGHT* WAY

Also at this point, it is worth considering (and with a friendly audience) how you are going to introduce the exercise. By this, we mean not the formal brief that the participants will receive, but what you will say prior to providing this. This is particularly important if your materials are home-made and lack the instant authority of a shop-bought package.[2]

Practitioner's Exercise

Consider the effect the following five introductions would have on you *as a learner*:

'Now, this next thing is just a bit of fun!'

'We're going to do an exercise which will test your communication skills to the limit.'

'In all of your performance reviews, you all needed huge improvement in your interpersonal skills so we've written a game to bring you up to scratch.'

'You all know that managing diversity is the biggest challenge facing our organization. This next hour will demonstrate where you're going wrong.'

'I'm sorry about this: it's new so I hope it will work…'

We have heard these, or variants of them, in real training situations and the effects are catastrophic. Even the best exercise can be undone by a poor warm-up.

Our experience is that the less said in setting up an activity, the better. The exercise should speak for itself and its purpose should be self-evident. In addition, if the experience has been well designed (see above) the participants' full engagement is far more likely and disengagement will have been mitigated against.

Reviewing and Improving Your Designs (5)

I am, as I am; whether hideous, or handsome, depends upon who is made judge.
Herman Melville (Writer)

---

2   On issues concerning trainer and training credibility, Alison Hardingham's *Psychology for Trainers* (1998) comes highly recommended.

After your activity has been piloted, take some time to revisit the Practitioner's Enquiries in the sections above. Don't give in to the temptation of judging an activity too soon; leave it for at least 24 hours before reflecting on your experience and objectively considering how the task/activity/exercise could or should be amended.

Even after a live run with a 'real' group, remember also that the purpose of any given intervention is almost certainly to effect a change in behaviour. As such, you may need some insight into how the learning has been embedded in reality before changing the exercise. *The proof of the pudding here is not in the eating but in the resulting energy and growth.*

Be sure, however, when reviewing the activity, that you do consider both the learning *objective* and the learning *object*.

REVIEW AND ADAPT THE OBJECT (5a)

If there were problems with the materials of the exercise, simulation or game, could you adapt the object (instructions/rules/materials) to achieve the objective? Or do you need to go back to the drawing board?

For instance, some years ago, I wrote a simulation where participants had to use sewing pins to join other components of the exercise together (I pretended they were steel beams in a scaled-down construction project). This had a number of flaws, not least the health and safety aspects, and the fact that it was difficult to collect them in and reuse them. The rest of the exercise was sound, and so I experimented with split pins, drawing pins and thumbtacks until I found a solution (straightened paperclips) that kept the integrity of the exercise while avoiding the logistical issues and bloody fingers.

REVIEW AND ADAPT THE OBJECTIVE (5b)

If the mechanics and logistics of the game worked but it didn't deliver the desired learning, could you just reconsider the objective and use the same game for a different purpose? For instance, a game that we designed to promote team cooperation and harmony in fact caused considerable conflict amongst the participants. With good quality review, this conflict gave rise to a valuable discussion which ultimately strengthened the team. We realized that the exercise had exposed key differences in the visions and values of the team members and so in future we used this exercise deliberately to promote discussion in these areas.

So far, we've spent a great deal of time and attention focusing on the materials, and what the learners may or may not be doing, and very little time focusing on what you as facilitator or trainer should be doing. So what *is* your role when the exercise is running?

> *When the best leader's work is done the people say, 'We did it ourselves!'*
> Attributed to Lao-Tsu (Chinese Philosopher)

TO BE PRESENT OR NOT

Should a facilitator necessarily be present during a group activity? Our feeling is that there are many factors at play that are affected by your presence. Whether you are merely in the corner of the room, or silently taking notes, or interjecting every two minutes or simply whether or not you are paying attention to what your participants are doing, all potentially have different impacts. The sole important concern however is:

Do you need to be present while your group does something in order to help them extract learning from it? And if so, how 'present' do you need to be? This section provides some thoughts and questions on this conundrum.

Option 1: Leave them alone

Facilitation of experiential learning is not about you. It is not about what *you* know, what *you* have seen, or about giving *you* an opportunity to try out *your* latest teaching technique or talk about the model *you* have just discovered. At its essence, we believe that our facilitation is concerned only with the participants' learning.

Being absent from an activity is a way of forcing oneself into a more facilitative frame of mind. You cannot be there, taking notes of who said what to whom and what the impact was in order to demonstrate your powers of observation in the review discussion. Instead you are relying on the participants' ability to tell you the important parts of what happened and to draw out for themselves what the impact was. It is a risk; yet it can be immensely powerful in terms of others' learning.

It also offers a marked opportunity for learning in that groups may well behave more realistically knowing that you're not there watching over them like some Orwellian sentinel. However, concerns over whether a group can be trusted to behave ideally and keep the right focus may well outweigh the benefits of group independence.

Option 2: Be fully immersed

If you choose to remain during the activity so that you are able to see what took place, be sure to be alert to *all* that is going on.

Listen to what is being said – to *exactly* what is being said. Who came up with an idea first? Who said, 'I have an idea' but was completely ignored? Who is checking that everyone is committed to the activity? Listening and observing while the group are engaged in a task is fundamental in helping a group to successfully unpack the learning experience *after* the event. Picking up what is really important to an individual member involves listening not just to the words being said, but to the tone of voice and, sometimes, to what is *not* being said as well. Any one of these cues can be vital to pick up and the skilled facilitator will focus on exactly the right word or phrase if they are listening well.

Notice what you feel. Not in terms of physical sensation so much (although this may sometimes be relevant) but in terms of your sense of how things are going. Prepare observations based on these feelings too, so later you can offer these as catalysts for discussion; such as: 'So, I started to feel a bit uncomfortable when X happened, how did any of the rest of you feel? What was going on then?' If you are honest with your own feelings and reactions, the impact will almost always be positive.

What is the 'elephant in the room,' the subject which the participants are not addressing? Sometimes there is a glaring concern that emerges during a task and this, for whatever reason, does not get mentioned by the group. Be ready to address the big issue at the end of the exercise, or maybe to interject while the exercise is 'live'.

When to speak and when to be silent

If a group is getting the exercise 'wrong', should you interrupt them? What are the pros and cons of interfering with a group who are in the middle of an activity?

If the group are struggling, an intervention can help them get started again, and may well facilitate real learning. On the other hand, often our pivotal learning comes as a result of our failures. There may well be multiple routes through an exercise and a group may have creatively found an unforeseen hidden path, interrupting them to tell them the right way can crush this entrepreneurship, however, they may just be collectively wasting each other's time. Before you speak, count to ten and consider the following questions:

Practitioner's Enquiries

Should a group be allowed to fail and sink splendidly or would a little swimming lesson help?

What effect will it have on the group dynamic if I butt in?

What effect will my intervention have on task progress?

How can I make an interjection in a neutral and not a leading way?

How bad is it *really* if they fail?

Am I interjecting because of an attachment to my game, or because I have their learning as my prime concern?

Will my interjections benefit only one or many learners?

Could I interject in a more subtle way? (Sometimes a well-timed cough or glance can be sufficient.)

As a further note of caution, there is a mammoth difference between asking a group: 'Are you sure that's correct?' and saying 'You don't want to do it like that, you want to do it like this!' and showing off the 'right' answer. Be careful that your interjections are timed well and neutral insofar as the task is concerned.

During a task, a group may ask questions of you. You need to think very quickly but very carefully about whether you answer them, how you answer them and what effect your answers will have. If the exercise is well tested there should be no need to answer task-clarification questions and the rebuttal 'Everything you need is in the brief' should suffice. However, occasionally clarification is required and so ensure you do so in a way which maintains the integrity of your exercise and the independency of the group.

Another, final, possibility for the physically-present facilitator is the creation of a timeline which can then be used to stimulate discussion. This could provide a note of any events of interest: the time when the first encouraging comment was made; the time when the most reticent group member contributed; duration of a planning phase; periods of silence and so forth.

Option 3: Both present and absent – start and finish

Having described the two possibilities, it is clear that a third option exists, that is, that the facilitator is present for the start and the finish of the task, possibly with a short visit during the course of the activity as well. This allows you to develop an impression of what has been taking place, a 'feel' for how the group has been working, but without so much information that you are tempted to take over during the review discussion.

After providing your impressions from your sampled moments, a useful conversation can ensue based on the participants providing missing information, or discussing how the task and the team, as well as each individual, had developed in your absence.

Regardless of your personal preference, two things should steer your actions:

First, that the group should understand exactly what your role is. This is sometimes obvious, but sometimes needs explaining. For instance, telling a group that 'Everything you need to know is on the brief; and I'll be back in five to see how you're getting on' is very different to simply leaving the room.

Second, the major focus again must always be on their learning, not your comfort.

*****

This part provided a general and theoretical underpinning of the design, set-up and running of artificial experiential learning activities. As we mentioned at the start of the chapter, the real learning comes in the extraction, translation and transformation of these experiences. The art of facilitating these transformations and conversations is dealt with in the next section of the book.

I am always willing to learn. I do not, however, always enjoy being taught.
Winston Churchill (Statesman)

The Skills of Facilitation

CHAPTER

2 *Extracting the Lesson: How to Review, Capture and Amplify the Learning*

Experience is not what happens to you. It is what you do with what happens to you.

Aldous Huxley (Writer)

When I worked in a Human Resources department, one of my colleagues commented on a job application: 'It says he's had seven years' experience. But my question is this: has he really had seven years' experience, or has he had one year of experience seven times?'

Events happen. Parties, accidents, great days, bad days and training days. We learn not by exposing ourselves to events, but by truly experiencing them and by consciously extracting the learning from what has happened and our responses to what has happened.

More than a Game: Reviewing a Learning Activity

Whilst in the care of his mother, two-year old Peter shuts his little finger in a door. There proceeds a good deal of wailing and some clearing up but, when the tears have subsided, his mother has one question: '*What could, or should, I have done differently?*'

The injury is not serious, so the experience provides a great opportunity for her to learn. She examines her actions and reactions, then looks at the impact of these on her son's physical and emotional wellbeing; and then, crucially, considers making changes in the future. In a real sense, she learned from the experience.

By its nature, artificial experiential learning does not involve the pain of trapped fingers. However, Peter's mother had the right idea. If your activity is to be valuable, it must not remain simply an activity, an event that happened to a group of people. The experience needs to be mined, distilled, condensed and reduced for real learning to take place.

Facilitation (fa–cil–i–**ta**–tion) noun   The act of making easy or easier.

So what can you do to help your activities become truly more than a game? What can you do to facilitate the learning process? What do your group need in order to help them maximize the impact of any training intervention and how could you help them to complete the cycles of learning set out in the opening sections of this book? In this chapter we offer some core principles, tips and questions that you'll find priceless when reviewing any activity, or indeed real performance on a day-to-day basis. We'll also consider how everyday objects may help the review process.[1]

Focus on the Learning

In order to keep a discussion grounded and focused, remember that the end focus must always be on what is being learned. 'The Learning' should be a stake that pins the discussion down and stops it travelling off on to intriguing but irrelevant tangents. If you have not been present during the activity, the temptation can be very strong for participants to tell you in detail what happened that outraged/enthralled them. The key to maintaining focus here is to notice when you're being told a story rather than being provided with context for learning. Sentences such as those that begin 'And then...' are a sure sign of a story being told. In order to keep on track, don't be afraid to ask 'So what?' or 'What was the impact of that?' This will encourage the participant speaking to distil the learning from an event and provide one or two key lessons from an activity. This is a useful exercise for them and for the other participants.

An effective review will have three elements to it, namely:

*   What happened?
*   So what?
*   Now what?

This is exemplified below.

What happened? Peter trapped his fingers in a door of his house.

So what? Small children are curious, doors are interesting and his mother had turned her back, because she couldn't watch him constantly.

Now what? Realizing the impossibility of constant vigilance, Peter's mother invests in a door cushion to prevent the door closing fully.

The 'What happened?' element is simply to provide a reference point and some context to the learning from the incident which takes place in the 'So what?' phase. 'Now what?' allows the learning to be distilled into a potential behaviour change for the future. The first phase is the easiest – participants don't have to reflect, but simply to report. A certain amount of this is helpful in providing context, but do move on quickly to the more productive 'So what?' and 'Now what?' phases.

We have noticed that, in our own review discussions and in others' that we have heard stories of, a sure sign of an unproductive review is when the facilitator is dominating the discussion. When you realize that you are speaking more than any of the participants, it is time to make a conscious decision to shut up and hand the responsibility for the learning back to them.

Before moving on to the next activity, there is enormous value in providing an opportunity for the participants to summarize their learning so start a process of

---

1   For a really comprehensive account of what it takes to facilitate and lead learning reviews, we find both Roger Schwarz's book *The Skilled Facilitator* (2002) and Phil Clements and Tony Spinks' *A Practical Guide to Facilitation Skills: A Real-World Approach* (1993) to be hugely impressive and helpful works.

transferable planning. Simply asking them what behaviours they are going to start adopting, what are they going to stop and what are they going to continue provides a summary of what is important and moves the focus to the next task or activity whilst acknowledging the last.

How Much Time?

Don't skimp on the review. It's through this discussion, centred on a shared activity, that experiential learning comes into its own. However, the review, as with all activities discussed here, is about the learning. Plan your review strategy carefully. Think of all the possible areas that you could explore, and then limit yourself to the ones that provide the most potentially powerful lessons. After all, there's only so much that any person can take in at one time. Rather than us provide an absolute figure of what proportional time to assign to a task review it's far better for you to trust your gut instinct, seek feedback, ask your learners and never be afraid of co-facilitation with another trainer. All of these methods will help you to gauge what is an opportunity wasted, what is just right, and what is overkill. However, as a pointer; staying out of the 'What?' as much as possible and delving into the 'So what?' and the 'Now what?' will give a much more profitable return.

Once the learning has been extracted, it is time to move on. If you are prone to overdoing discussion or to indulging tangents, imposing a shorter time limit on your review can help to focus on the learning and provide a more efficient review.

Ten Top Learning Review Strategies

Give a man a fish and you feed him for a day. Teach a man to fish and you feed him for a lifetime.

Chinese Proverb

One key mistake that many novice trainers and facilitators make is that they dominate a learning conversation to the point where the group simply abrogate responsibility. The natural extension of this situation is that when the learners return to 'business as usual' they are unable to transfer some of the learning in the absence of the teacher.

An easy way to notice whether you're falling into this trap is to mentally chart the patterns of discourse in a group discussion. If every question is asked by you and every answer is directed to you, you may want to read on and reassess your technique.

By empowering the group to distil learning from an exercise themselves, which often means you saying less, you will inevitably help each individual to become more actively involved in their own learning. This has two powerful benefits in that an individual will take the learning from your intervention into their day-to-day experience and will be better equipped to learn from any experience.

In essence, you're empowering them to learn.

To help you to do this, here are our ten most useful strategies for facilitating a group learning review.

STRATEGY 1: GETTING THE CLIMATE RIGHT

Great learning starts before the formal learning experience starts. What can you do to ensure that the group is ready to learn? What can you do to ensure their self-comfort and intellectual safety? As freelancers with years of experience in facilitating departmental away-days, we estimate that we'll only end up working on the programme that we designed about 30 per cent of the time. Usually, the brief given by our contact has glossed over a massive issue that is obvious the moment the group enter the room. At that point, we usually decide that it's far better to do some work around that issue than it is to jolly a room full of un-jolly people into playing what they will inevitably see as an irrelevant game. (And perhaps it's a personal style thing, but starting an exercise with, 'Now, let's just start with something a bit fun' is a crime. Telling people they are going to have fun will ensure that they won't.) Simple things like agreeing confidentialities at the start and learning and using people's names can reap enormous returns and goodwill from even the most cynical of groups. And if they are aware from the start that you are taking their learning seriously, they will be more disposed to do the same.

STRATEGY 2: IT'S NOT ALL ABOUT YOU!

Remember, you're not a teacher; you're there to facilitate learning. So leave your preconceptions about the group and the activities at the door. If they learn the lesson you intended, fantastic. If they didn't, then they *will* have got something else. We advise new facilitators to start any review with:

'So, how was that?'

and then stand well back; as generally in an experiential setting the more you talk, the less they'll learn.

We've seen many trainers and facilitators try to rescue a dud experience by telling the group what they *should* have learned. It never works. Your job here is to maximize the value of what they *did* learn; not to attempt to implant false memories.

During the exercise your focus, at all times, needs to be on what *actually* happened – not what *should* have happened.

STRATEGY 3: NOTICING AND PRESENTING DATA – NOT OPINION

As a reviewer and facilitator of learning, your job is to *really* pay attention if you are in the room. I facilitated a group review some years ago where we based an hour-long crucial conversation on a slightly raised eyebrow. The team leader (and real-life boss) had insisted on a course of action. One of the team at this point flicked one eyebrow up one centimetre for no more than a second. As a facilitator, I didn't yet know what this gesture meant – it was just data. But it was noted. After the exercise I steered the conversation around to the decision which resulted in the raised brow.

The boss asserted that, 'Everyone had agreed on that decision' which I didn't think was true. But, rather than say, 'I don't think that everyone agreed' I simply looked straight at the eyebrow raiser, raised *my* eyebrow and said, 'So, everyone agreed...' and let the sentence hang for a moment. And another. And another.

Eventually, the eyebrow raiser spoke up, 'Well, no...I didn't...really agree...'

And then from the rest of the group out poured a torrent of, 'Well, actually...' and 'Yeah, me neither...'

The original learning points of the exercise were then jettisoned completely, as the conversation about why the (very friendly and nice) boss had been able to dominate in spite of everyone's silent objections was a far more productive route for the long term.

In the fields of observation chance favours only the prepared mind.

Louis Pasteur (Scientist)

So, pay attention to what you see, hear and feel, and don't be afraid to blurt out what you 'noticed'. Make it safe by following it with a curious (in tone and spirit) question, like so:

'After five minutes, I noticed a definite increase in volume and sharpness of tone. What was *that*?'

As opposed to:

'You just started getting irate with each other. Why was that?'

Practitioner's Enquiries

Would it be helpful to watch for who picks up the brief and who starts straight on the materials?

Could you note how long before they clarify the objective, at what point did they draw up a plan, where did the plan get thrown away, how long before they mentioned timings and so on?

Did they move the furniture or layout so that everyone could see?

If a new group, did they use names?

Did they encourage each other and praise?

Did they acknowledge each other's ideas when building upon them?

Would it serve your thinking to draw up a timeline of these processes, to show to the group?

What signs could you watch for to give evidence of individual/team engagement and disengagement from task, team and process?

Are you observing facial expression, body language and posture?

Are you really paying attention to the tonality, and audible collegiality of the group?

Who deferred to whom? (In the face of a 'new' learning experience, there's not necessarily a right and wrong way to engage with a task. So any deferral without explicit rationale is ripe for a learning conversation after the event.)

The 'irate with each other' is *your* inferred opinion, not factual noticed data. Stick to the facts and just the facts.

Create your own mental checklist of things to notice, but essentially stay alert, focused and ensure that your attention (from a safe distance) stays on the group, and not your agenda.

Make observations and then allow the participants to interpret them. If you have noticed someone's reaction, comment on the behaviour rather than what you assume to be the underlying emotion. 'So Chris, when X happened, I noticed that you sat back and folded your arms. What was going on for you then?' This gives Chris the *opportunity* to discuss what they were feeling at that point, which could be resignation, confusion, thoughtfulness, frustration or almost anything else.

Finally here, don't be afraid to name the elephant in the room. If there is something that needs to be said, then say it, or alternatively tell the group that there's something obvious that they're dodging as an issue. Don't be attached to your insight and give the group opportunity to respond to it. A facilitator is not a member of the group in the same way and so can therefore be free to raise these issues by asking bold questions.

STRATEGY 4: PAY ATTENTION TO THE ROLES PEOPLE TAKE

In any exercise which has teamwork, leadership, communications or process management at its core, it is worth paying attention to the generic roles and behaviours that people take. Understanding these can help the process of translation back into daily life. For instance, running out of time on a training-room exercise is really no big deal, but if the reason for this is that no one paid attention to process management *just like back in the office* then there can be some interesting avenues of learning opened up here. Moreover, it is important to ensure that the group has a shared understanding of the generic roles that they are exhibiting, so that the group can take these conversations and concepts more easily into the processing and planning of other, and more real, activities.

There are a huge number of team roles models and all of them offer certain similarities and certain differences. We both were professionally raised using the Belbin® Team Roles Model.[2] This model, which is widely used and understood by many organizations, has huge value. Our experience, however, is that it needs careful management and skilled teaching, as some participants can, after completing the diagnostic questionnaire, find themselves feeling that they have been assigned a life-long role. This perceived assignation of roles can detract from an individual's creativity, flexibility and responsibility. We have both heard group members express feelings such as: 'Don't ask me how to manage this, I'm just the ideas person,' or even 'You can't be offended by my bluntness, that's my role.' The focus that the Belbin® model places on roles over behaviour, if left unchallenged, can allow people to hide and can inhibit people from behaving in a way that might be seen as 'untypical'. Remember that, whichever model or diagnostic you use to explain behaviours and roles, you need to have thought carefully about why you are using it and to consider the intent behind the tool's design. The intent behind the Belbin® model is certainly not to pigeon-hole people – even though this is the effect that it can sometimes have if not carefully applied.

---

2   See: http://www.belbin.com/.

An elegant and simple model which we both value is the Four Player System, based on the work of David Kantor and William Lehr, from their book *Inside the Family* (1975). This first came to prominence as a work designed to examine and explain family dynamics, but has more recently come to be used for analyzing the structural balance in work-based teams.[3]

The Four Player model asserts that four core acts are the essential building blocks of both dysfunctional and healthy team behaviour. They are 'mover', 'follower', 'opposer' and 'bystander'; and can be best captured with the following typical sentiments.

Mover: Without a 'mover' in a group or team, there is no impetus to act or make a decision. For instance, 'Let's do X. It's clear that X is the best course of action.'

Of course, not every decision will be uncontested and in an experiential setting where there are no hierarchies, often the facilitator will be able to observe a power struggle between the 'mover' and the challenger. Kantor and Lehr (1975) call this challenger the 'opposer'.

Opposer: The 'opposer' function plays a vital role in team dynamics as without any opposition there can be no checking of the validity of a leader's view. For instance: 'No, I disagree. X is the wrong thing to do; we'll run out of time if we do X.'

In any team there will also be individuals who are engage with the task in a different way. Kantor and Lehr call these 'followers' and 'bystanders'.

Follower: 'Movers' or leaders need 'followers' as without them decisions cannot be implemented. For instance, 'I agree. X is the right course of action. I'll get started on it.'

The counterpoint to a 'follower' is the individual who neither wishes to lead or oppose an action or decision.

Bystanders: The 'bystanding' role provides perspective and evaluation of the process and performance. For instance: 'Hang on a minute, we tried this approach before and it didn't work then. What's changed?'

A balance of these behaviours will occur in any healthy team, and an imbalance will result in issues and problems of sorts. As such, as a reviewer you need to be observing and listening for behaviours that indicate in some way decisive leadership, followership, opposition and the perspective that a bystander will give. It's important to realize that the bystanding function is not disengagement, but something potentially far more useful to the group, provided that it is channelled and used in the right way.

It is also worth noting the potential conflicts between movement and opposition, followership and bystanding. Again, allowing the team space to work through any conflicts or storms here can result in powerful learning. Of course, these roles can switch constantly depending on a huge variety of factors – all the more reason for you to be in the room with all your senses working. Helping teams and individuals to realize and understand the types of behaviours that they typically each demonstrate can give them huge insight into how as a team they can improve their performance.

---

3   See Kantor and Lehr (1975) for the original, and Ancona and Isaacs (2006) for a work-based application.

Practitioner's Enquiries

What are the generic roles being taken by the individuals in your teams?

What are the conflicts between the roles taken?

Who leads, follows, questions, clarifies, acknowledges action, ensures wellbeing, drives performance, thinks creatively, monitors resource and so on?

Are the roles and behaviours balanced? Are there too many conflicting leaders, for example?

How does the balance of generic roles taken emulate the group's real-world makeup?

STRATEGY 5: ASK FEWER, MORE POWERFUL QUESTIONS

Page one of the trainers' and facilitators' fictional handbook probably contains a paragraph on the difference between open and closed questions, and why you should ask the former and avoid the latter. In our experience, the power of a question is less to do with the *type* of question and more to do with the *intent* behind it. Think about the biggest, most challenging question that personally you've ever been asked. You'll probably notice that the question is short and might be either a 'What' question (that is, 'What do you *really* want?') or a 'Why' question (that is 'Why are you *here*?'). Either way these questions are powerful because they contain three essential components:

a)   Short – don't use twenty words when five will do.
b)   Open – keep the conversation alive and avoid the possibility of a yes/no response.
c)   Personal – they're aimed at an individual personally, or to the group as an entity (not purely academically interesting).

When to ask 'Why?' and when to ask 'What?'

'Why?' questions tend to focus an individual or group on diagnostic internalization. For instance 'Why did you make that poor decision?' is potentially an interesting question. However, if your intent is to have the group actively considering how they could use this experience in the future then, 'So, what's going to ensure you don't make a similar decision in a similar situation?' might have more power. Practise your questions in both why and what forms until you're fluent with both. If in doubt, use a future-focused 'What?' as this tends to focus a conversation towards positive action. For instance:

What was the learning at that point?

What can you take from that (good/bad) decision?

If you were to repeat that, what would have been a more successful outcome/output?

In order for any learning review to work effectively, it is essential that you get at the *honesty* in a group.

STRATEGY 6: GETTING AT THE HONESTY

Generally people say they want honesty, in their leaders, their colleagues and their friends. But consider how often honesty is sacrificed on the altar of diplomacy and tact. We say the professional thing, the polite thing, the thing that won't upset or offend and in reality this veneer is completely understandable.

However, in an artificial situation there is potential scope for more honesty as here learning can take precedence over social niceties.

Getting at the honesty in a group is partly to do with getting the climate right (see above) but also to do with ensuring a means or conduit for people to tell the truth without reprisal and in a long-term helpful way. Often dishonesty comes when a group member dilutes their position in the face of unintentional social pressure. For instance, if the dialogue goes unchallenged, a team review of a 'successful' task can sound like this.

Facilitator:	'So, how was that?'
Team Member (TM) #1:	'Great!'
TM #2:	'Fantastic!'
TM #3:	'Really good!!'

Now, TM #4 has had a torrid time of things. They've been marginalized and the group took several decisions that TM #4 didn't agree with. However, the task has been executed successfully, and in the light of this and the exaltations of the rest of the team, TM #4 is likely to respond thus:

TM #4:	'Pretty good.'
or	
TM #4:	'Good...I suppose.'

(Or any other platitude designed to fit in, and not undermine what has been a 'successful' operation.)

If left unchallenged, this type of conversation probably renders the exercise irrelevant. Yes the group built the tallest tower out of clothes-pegs, but they did it in a way that marginalized at least part of their team. A short-term victory, but (if recreated in real life) possibly a long-term problem.

Since you, as learning facilitator, are paying attention to the *process* as well as the *task*, you could probably step in and challenge at this point, (for instance, 'I notice that there just seems to be a discrepancy between TM #1, 2, 3 and 4...') and this is certainly a valid tactic. However, if your purpose is to have the group function independently of you (and let's face it, this is surely the point of *any* teaching intervention), are there other ways that you could get to the same realization?

Politeness often avoids real honesty due to the fear of damaging a relationship. However, when honest feedback and open discourse are associated with progress in a learning environment, that positive association may be carried into the real world.

Learning environments can provide a safer space to receive challenging feedback or to have an open conversation, simply because there is less at stake.

The avoidance of honesty takes several forms. In order to be polite, or possibly from less honourable motives whether conscious or subconscious, participants in a group activity will tend to be selective in what they choose to say. They will delete events from the collective memory by simply excluding the reporting of them. If nobody mentions Martin slamming his mug down on the table, it didn't happen.

One only needs to consider the oft-reported difficulty that the police have with multiple witness reports of the same incident to know that people will have their own perception of an event. This can lead to a distortion of the truth. Our experience suggests that a vocal member of a group will frequently state afterwards, 'We all contributed the same' whereas the same discussion will be reported in a very different light by the group member who was not able to make their opinion heard.

The other tendency that participants have in this setting is to generalize their experience and project it on to all. 'Everyone knew exactly what the plan was,' 'We all thought this idea was the best' or 'No one understood the problem for ages' are representative of the ways people will generalize. One problem with this is that the 'generalized' group members may feel uncomfortable contradicting the 'generalizer' thus feeling unable then to express their own, alternative, experience.

Honest dialogue can be initially difficult but can result in marked progress in the long term, provided that all concerned are party to the new rules of engagement.

Susan Scott's *Fierce Conversations* (2003) identifies seven principles which underlie conversations 'in which we come out from behind ourselves into the conversation and make it real'. These principles (paraphrased here) represent for us the essence of an honest review:

- **Interrogate reality** – we are constantly changing; interrogating what is actually happening will reduce the number of erroneous assumptions clouding the communication.
- **Make it real** – if people lay down their masks and communicate with each other rather than with each other's presented personas, the conversations are increasingly effective.
- **Be present in the conversation** – communicate as if this is the most significant conversation you will ever have, rather than as if there were three more interesting places to be.
- **Tackle the toughest challenge** – name the biggest issue and then work on solving it together. This will prevent the same issues causing stumbles again and again.
- **Obey your instincts** – pay attention to your sense of what is occurring and share those impressions with others.
- **Take responsibility for repercussions** – increased honesty can result in bluntness. If you can practise sharing your honest thoughts in a way that is palatable for others to hear, less time will be spent mopping up.
- **Allow silence** – many insights are lost because of the distractions in incessant speech. Giving breathing space can allow people to process what they are hearing and experiencing the impact of the conversation fully.

Often, honesty and open discourse is rendered a near-impossibility by the agenda of the trainer or manager. If the group believes that they are being judged or monitored or that you are dogmatically after the 'right' answer then this is what they will attempt to give you. In order to get at the honesty when you genuinely have an agenda, it may be necessary to explicitly suspend this for a while. Often it is sufficient to do this by simply stating the obvious, for example, 'OK, we all know that as a manager I'm concerned about maximizing profit; but let's put that to one side for the time being and talk about the other issues at stake.'

Three Quick Honesty-Generators That Work

i) The 'big reveal'

Have the participants privately score their performance before any review. This can be quantitatively (a score out of ten on a sticky note), or qualitatively (a one-word summary of performance on a card). The 'big reveal' comes when as you say '1, 2, 3…reveal' and the individuals display and read out their innermost thoughts. It works because of the privacy of the fact that no one knows what anyone else will write, so they write what is true, not what is easy. Typical 'big reveals' often sound like this as participants read out their assessments '9…8…9…10…4…9' or 'Efficient…Professional…Slick…*Shambolic*'. The discrepancies here are obvious and the group will then do much of the learning without you. This can be adapted for almost any learning experience.

'In one word, how do you feel about that issue?'

'Out of ten, how likely is that strategy to work in reality?'

'Percentage-wise, how likely are you to implement that back in the office?'

ii) Milk-bottle tops – stop, start, continue

Start collecting red, green and blue milk-bottle tops (or different coloured tiddlywinks or poker chips). These can represent feedback prompts and can provide a tactile and potentially powerful way of helping people to say what they really need to.

We often use a 'stop, start, continue'-style of learning review. We find this to be generally helpful as it allows teams or individuals to focus on a negative action or behaviour that they will cease; something that they need to start doing and something effective that they will continue to do. The milk-bottle top colours make handy, tactile reminders of these actions, as well as resembling a currency that can physically be transferred between members. A red top signifies 'stop', a green signifies 'start' and a blue signifies 'continue'.

iia) Basic stop, start, continue milk-bottle top review

Place all of the tops in a pile in the centre and each member has to take turns to take a counter and disclose either a 'stop', 'start' or a 'continue' for themselves, for the group or for the task at hand.* Continue until all the counters have been removed or the conversation has taken an interesting turn. (You may want to build in rules that throughout the review each team member has to take equal proportions of red, green and blue tokens.)

A variety of this review method is to restrict the stop, start, continue topic of conversation to be either 'task' (that is, in the next project we will budget more efficiently), 'team' (that is, we need to start being clear what we each contribute) or an 'individual' (that is, I need to make sure I listen to Sam).

iib) Milk-bottle top success/not success review

Where tasks are being successfully implemented, teams sometimes cannot articulate *why* they are successful. This makes replicating the success very difficult when team members change.

In this case review in the same style as above, but change the number of counters in the centre so there are more stops (red) and starts (green) than continues (blue). This encourages a challenging and constructively critical mentality and helps work-teams to be honest and avoid complacency.

Conversely, when a task has 'failed', learners often focus on the failure ('We failed to build a marshmallow and spaghetti bridge...' which is, on a day-to-day basis, irrelevant) and ignore all of the good and positive things that came from the experience.

Where a team has not worked well, or suffered a project setback, it can be easy for reviews to descend into a blaming session – either directed at external or internal factors. While some conflict can be helpful it is often helpful as a facilitator or manager to steer the conversation on to maintaining the positives. Review in the same style as above but increase the number of blue (continue) counters.

In our experience, many organizational cultures do not encourage peer feedback, and certainly it is difficult to offer commentary 'upwards' in the organization. Often groups need a little help with giving honest feedback.

iii) Quantity first – Then quality

Issue each member of a group with a number of tokens of some sort. We typically use playing cards, the ubiquitous milk-bottle tops, sweets, pasta shapes, paper clips or anything that is small, tactile and can be found lying around in a stationery cupboard. The important thing is that you need lots (at least ten per group member). The concept is simple: give each member a stack of tokens and every time he or she offers a new comment they 'lose' a token. When they're out of tokens they have only to listen. This is rather like the conch shell in Golding's *Lord of the Flies*, only in reverse. It encourages the quieter members to participate equally and illustrates who is dominating continually. By using a large number of counters the obvious comments are dispensed with quickly and groups are required to be more creative, insightful, challenging and honest in what they say.

You can add variety to this type of review by adding different types of characteristics to different types of tokens. For example, recently, I ran a team away day and wanted them to be more honest with each other. I used pasta shapes in this form of review where fusili (twists) represented confusion, penne (tubes) represented a telescope for clarity and conchiglie (shells) represented secrecy (things they would say if they came out of their shell). This kind of activity may appear contrived, but set up unapologetically it allowed the group to say some things that had been festering for some time.

An additional resource that we also find useful here is the *Feedback Game©*. This resource, developed by Peter Gerrickens (1998), comprises a series of feedback cards which can be played in a variety of ways to encourage honesty and disclosure. It is often a key addition to my essential bag of kit illustrated earlier.

Note: * A handy model that can be employed here is John Adair's Functional Leadership over-lapping circles model of Task, Team, Individual. See Adair (2006) or the Leadership and Teamwork chapters (Chapters 3 and 4) in this book for more information.

STRATEGY 7: DEALING WITH TASK-BLAMING

No matter how well you have constructed any artificial learning experience, and no matter how realistic it is (from a simple energizing ice-breaker to a multi-million pound flight simulator), there is still some possibility that learners can level the challenge of unrealism against your exercise. This is especially likely if the exercise wasn't challenging enough ('...but real life is harder/more stressful/more complex' and so on) or that a group 'failed' in the execution of the task ('...but we didn't have enough time'). This can be referred to as 'blaming the task'. Groups will frequently abrogate responsibility for their own performance on to the exercise or scenario, and it is hence vital to:

* note their concerns and, if valid, use them in any redesigns;
* focus the attention back on the learning gained as even a disastrous performance or a poor task can be a useful source of learning if reviewed well.

The phrase, '...but this wasn't real' is an clear indicator of someone blaming the task, and cries out for someone to point out that it was 'real' *because it did just happen*, and to steer the conversation back to the learning. However, if you designed the intervention well, then these concerns do not often arise. Another helpful tactic is to intimate that the exercise was written to be an authentic representation of their real situations and to ask the group what similarities they noticed. Often the things that a group finds in an exercise are better than the initial designed outcomes!

STRATEGY 8: DEALING WITH DIFFICULT CONVERSATIONS

The author C.S. Lewis once wrote: 'Experience: that most brutal of teachers. But you learn, my God do you learn.' If people are honest with one another, these learning experiences and conversations can be brutal. It is sometimes not easy to face the impact you have had on your colleagues; to have a mirror held up to your behaviour. It is in these hard reviews where the skilled facilitator and reviewer can come into their own.

Learning conversations often get heated and all good review groups will have times where the conversation gets challenging. This happens most often when a participant behaves in a negative or unhelpful manner. Facilitators often respond to, and end up arguing with, the difficult individual in question. The group's conversation then becomes a displaced confrontation, and opportunities for learning are lost.[4] Here are some tell-tale signs to watch out for and some solutions that we find helpful in avoiding or defusing the issue.

Little ol' us

Problem: The group says to you: 'What do *you* think?'/'What *should* we be doing?'/'What's the *best* way to do it?'/'*You're* the expert, you tell us…'

Solution: Once you start to tell a group or individual the answers, solutions or methods, you may as well not have bothered with the exercise in the first place. Furthermore, they'll then start to look to you at every turn and abrogate responsibility for their learning.[5] It is thus essential that you don't answer this question directly.

Being able to deflect questions is a useful skill which can facilitate great amounts of learning. 'What do *you* think we did well?' can be deflected simply with 'What do *you* think I'm going to say?' but this strategy only lasts for so long. Practise only answering a question with another question until you can deflect questions and reflect the learning back onto the group with seamless skill.

Blamestorming

Problem: (One faction of a learning group are talking about another faction.) 'They did [x] and it's their fault that we never meet our deadlines.'

Solution: Steer the focus away from 'they' and 'their' and on to how the specific individual in question feels or is affected: 'Sounds like you're having hard time. So how could you respond productively when they do [x]?'

Generalisms

Problem: 'No-one ever listens to me!'

Solution: Request specificity as 'No one *ever* listens to me' is unlikely to be wholly accurate. 'Could you give us a specific example so we can understand?'

---

4   When dealing with difficult conversations there is much here that can be learned from the field of social care, for example Ron Kraybill's *Facilitating Facilitation* (1994). Also worth reading are *Crucial Conversations* (Patterson et al., 2002) and *Difficult Conversations* (Stone et al., 1999), as both offer helpful insight and tools for talking to people when the temperature is running high.

5   If ever I am tempted to show off my knowledge in an experiential setting, I am reminded of a friend of mine whose medical degree was largely based around problem-based learning. At the opening lecture, the head of the medical school stepped up to the lectern and told the anxious student doctors, 'I hope that each and every one of you realizes that this is a Fo-Fo course.' and with that he paused to let his wisdom sink in. Eventually a brave hand was raised and asked, 'Sorry, what do you mean, Fo-Fo?' 'A Fo-Fo course,' replied the teacher, 'stands for F*** Off and Find Out.' It is important that your exercises give participants the space to Fo-Fo, but that the process is designed to provide just the right level of boundary.

Loaded questions

Problem (addressed to you): 'Wouldn't you agree that he shouldn't have done that without at least asking us?'

    Solution: Whether you agree or not is entirely irrelevant. Reflecting it back on to the speaker may be more helpful. For instance, 'Sounds like you thought it was unprofessional?'

Withdrawing

Problem: Participant says '...'.

    Solution: If a group member has said very little for a long time and whose body language is screaming disengagement, you need to ensure either: that the member gets a personal chance to contribute ('X, is there anything that you'd like to offer?'); or, better, that the group remedy this themselves (that is, 'I'm noticing that there's a real imbalance of contribution at the moment...is that usual?').

    I was working with a group recently that had a member who would withdraw at any available opportunity. I introduced a peer-feedback exercise and I was delighted when one of the other members addressed the withdrawer's frequent absence directly: 'Sometimes, you're really "here" and your contribution is fantastic. But sometimes it seems you're just not interested. Is there anything we can do to help you be "here" more often?' The problem was exposed as a whole group issue; and the withdrawer was confronted with the impact of his behaviour in a way that made it easy for him to learn.

Ventriloquism

Problem: Participant says 'What X is trying to say is that everyone thinks that we should do more than pay lip service to this agenda.'

    Solution: When one group member speaks on behalf of another (ventriloquism), it's essential that you let the original member express their opinions (for example, 'I'd really like to hear X tell us personally'). Also, note the generalization in the ventriloquist's interruption: 'everyone thinks' in this situation actually means 'I think'.

Over-talking

Problem: In the middle of conversation, group member X says, 'I just don't think that we...' Group member Y then interrupts X with, 'What we need to be doing is telling them that...'

    Solution: The lack of respect shown by the over-talking here can't be healthy for a group in the long term. It's important that you don't belittle Y's comments, but at the same time make it clear that the behaviour is inappropriate and that X had a right to contribute. For instance, 'Y, that sounds interesting, but I'd rather not interrupt the point that X was making.' Ensure that you come back to Y's point in the future, and be consistent with your management of behaviour that you and the group consider to be inappropriate. If symptoms persist, it may be that all the group members find it perfectly acceptable to over-talk, and it's only you that objects. Still, a type of contracting conversation of what is appropriate, and what is not, might be an important part of establishing the right learning climate.

With all difficult situations (and indeed within any exercise that starts to go 'wrong') you will frequently be faced with the dilemma of whether to interrupt or not. If you interrupt, the focus starts to move to you, and away from the group. If you don't then certain vital aspects can be lost, and any resultant learning might be diminished. When choosing to intervene or not, be guided by this principle:

All of your interventions should maximize and facilitate the learning.
If it doesn't do this, then leave well alone.

STRATEGY 9: REFLECTING, SUMMARIZING AND MOVING FORWARD

If your exercise is well designed and the outcomes were clear, it is vital that these are not lost in the heat of debrief conversation. To this end, one of the key roles that you have as a learning facilitator is to help the groups capture their learning. You can do this by doing three essential things – reflecting, summarizing and helping groups to move forward.

Reflecting

Reflecting is taking an assertion, statement, sentence or thought from a participant and bouncing it back in a way that makes it more transferable or helpful. For instance:

X: 'We ran out of time *again*.'
You: 'So what I think you're saying is that you didn't learn from the mistakes you made before?'

Or...
You: 'So what I'm hearing is that you didn't have a clear method for managing your work processes. Is that right?'

Or even (and my personally preferred style): 'So, you *didn't learn anything* then?'

Notice that all of these are delivered in question form, and so are not a hard, fast and immutable fact. They're up for discussion, but allow the group to take a transferable lesson (that is, we might need to reflect more on what we do, or we might need a clear management process, or we might need to *actually learn*) from a specific exercise. Clever reflection can help to ensure that a learning outcome is met. Groups often don't have the Damascene moment of clarity until after the exercise completes, and while we frequently steer discussion using reflection and noticing we rarely, if ever, force the point.

Summarizing

Summarizing is simply ensuring that learning is captured in a meaningful way. Often this requires a few moments of scribbling on a flipchart, but could be as involved as giving the group five minutes to prepare a presentation to you of what they learned (try different forms of presentation, like a weather or stock market report, QVC advert or reality TV voiceover). In essence, the more you encourage a group to take responsibility for capturing what they've learned, the more valuable the intervention.

Moving forward

It is essential that a group leaves a learning experience with a clear sense of what they have learned, in a practical and pragmatic form that they can transfer on to another situation. This part of the review is where you can restate their captured learning and encourage them to action plan for any future similar experience, whether real or fictional.

STRATEGY 10: DO WHATEVER IS REQUIRED TO FACILITATE LEARNING

If facilitating a learning review is about making the learning process stronger, more embedded and easier, then that should be your whole focus. If you're concerned about whether the group like you, or whether you might cause short-term discord, then you may be missing opportunities. That is not to say that you should be deliberately provocative (especially if time is short), but by the same token you shouldn't be afraid to do what is necessary.

One of the finest training interventions I've ever witnessed was when I shadowed an outside facilitator on a graduate development programme. We'd both spent the day with a team who were performing pretty well and were full of excuses for why they'd not excelled. Since their performance was above average (they were completing tasks adequately) no one inside the group was challenging their thinking, processing and actions. It was obvious to us observers that there was a 'simmering undercurrent of something not quite right' and so the facilitator decided to act. He bawled them out in the style of a sergeant-major, and told them in no uncertain terms that he was sick of their excuses, and then left the room, banging the door behind him. The group sat in silence for a long, long time, and then started to blame the trainer. Eventually the silence, and the blamestorming passed and the group started to address the real issue of their merely-adequate performance. By the time the trainer returned they were deep into a hugely productive conversation and the trainer (who half an hour before had been demonized) was welcomed back with gratitude. He still made sure that he explained the reason for his actions though.

And so, do whatever it takes to make sure that groups extract the most learning from your interventions.

> *To do nothing is sometimes a good remedy.*
>
> Hippocrates (Physician)

Sometimes a kick in the pants for a group is great facilitation. Sometimes saying nothing is the right thing to do. Sometimes asking the group what they want is sensible. Sometimes telling them what they need is great facilitation. Sometimes taking a break is great facilitation. Sometimes leaving the room is best. Sometimes divisively getting at the honesty is the right thing to do. Sometimes – oh, the list is endless. And that's the point. Your job from here is to do whatever is necessary and right for the group at that moment in time.

A wise colleague once explained that facilitating a learning review is to be like a quality shampoo and conditioner. You act when you're needed and you don't act when you are not.

Learning *when* to act, and *when not to*, is where the theory stops and real experience begins.

From this point we'll look in greater depth at a variety of issues that organizations face on a day-to-day basis, and how the training and developmental needs raised by these issues can be powerfully addressed by experiential learning.

PART **III**

The Developer's Toolbox – Specific Issues and Tactics

A learning experience is one of those things that say, 'You know that thing you just did? Don't do that.'

Douglas Adams (Author and Satirist)

3 *Helping Teams Work*

Coming together is a beginning. Keeping together is progress. Working together is success.

Henry Ford (Industrialist)

In any profession, a truly solo worker is a rare commodity. Regardless of preference, or physical surroundings, the majority of people need to interact with others in the course of their work and this is frequently a source of difficulty. People have different working styles, motivations, personal agendas and understandings of the goal or goals of their working life. These differences can result in demotivation on an individual level, conflict at a group level and inefficiency on an organizational level; but differences can also provide enormous benefits in thinking and approach. It is not surprising, therefore, that most managers and supervisors talk about, and some genuinely recognize, at least in theory, the importance of working as a team.

Teamwork interventions are offered by a large variety of organizations, from military reservists to dedicated companies with their own facilities. Many of these provide opportunities for individuals to participate as well as every member of an existing team. Individuals might discover how they typically fit in to teams, and what their working preferences and optimal roles are; existing teams, however, might find ways to handle specific issues within their workplace.

'Away days' or residential programmes, without any external facilitation, allow people to become better acquainted with each other. This shared, different experience can add a dimension to working relationships. Going away together and having a (preferably enjoyable) encounter will, therefore, have a positive 'teambuilding' effect in itself. However, this effect is often short-lived as there is sometimes little that can be translated and applied to a workplace environment once the trip is over.

So what does this mean to the creative trainer? How useful an intervention is will depend on adopting the appropriate strategy; and the team themselves may not be able to articulate what the necessary approach is. Recently we were asked by a client to provide a teamwork session for a group of individuals who were about to start working together. When we asked if there were any particular issues, concerns or problems, the client's response was, 'Well, they just need some real teambuilding; something to help them work together as a team.' This kind of response is not unusual, so a little deeper investigation on the part of the facilitator is necessary.

In order to work effectively as a team, what are the necessary ingredients? We believe there are three essential components, namely:

- a shared purpose or meaningful *goal*, and a clear understanding of the process required to reach it;

- open, frequent, honest and useful *communication* about both the job at hand (human doing) and each individual's personal needs (human being);
- a shared understanding and appreciation of each team member's *contribution* and role within the team.

So, when we are asked to run a teamwork session, the first thing we do is ask some questions:

Practitioner's Enquiries

Who are the people that will be participating in the course?

Are there existing 'dynamics' issues that you should be aware of?

Are there any official or unofficial workplace line-management hierarchies that you need to be familiar with?

Is there a fundamental existing core of the team which is being/has been supplemented by new members?

Are they an existing team, or are they a team in waiting or simply a disparate group of individuals who want to learn about teamwork (as is often the case if you are facilitating a course, as opposed to an away day)?

Of the three components mentioned above (goal, communication, contribution), which is the one that needs to be focused upon?

How long is the overall period of development? This is particularly appropriate with an established or forming 'real' team, since often issues are raised in experiential settings that, if left unresolved and not skilfully dealt with, can have major ramifications on a team's day-to-day performance.

Once you have a good idea of what the session may involve, you can start developing session aims and outcomes.

Let's say, for the sake of argument, the aims of the session are: a) to introduce a new group to each other; and b) highlight some of the different ways that people work within group settings.

Teambuilding Models, Frameworks and Theoretical Foundations

I have met people for whom 'teamwork' or 'teambuilding' is synonymous with 'silly games'. I confess, I love working with teams in new surroundings, outside if at all possible, and the more planks and buckets of water that are involved the better. However, as we have already established, there is little developmental point to these exercises unless they are developed and run with learning foremost in the facilitator's mind. There are several concepts in the teamwork literature which I rely upon in developing teamwork sessions.

THE JOHARI WINDOW

Joseph Luft and Harry Ingham developed this model (Luft, 1969) as a tool to illustrate and improve self-awareness and understanding between group members. They suggested that an individual possesses information about themselves; some of which is known and some unknown, both to themselves and to the people around them, as shown in Figure 3.1.

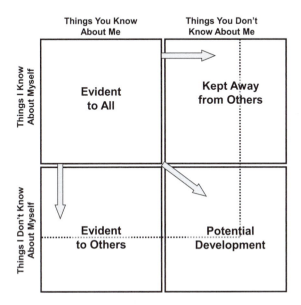

Figure 3.1   Adaptation of the Johari Window discovery model

Through shared experiences and feedback the 'open' area grows, reducing the relative size of the 'hidden' and 'blind' areas. Almost as a consequence of this, the 'unknown' area shrinks as an individual allows themselves to be encouraged and challenged into realizing their potential. This is why often teamwork sessions will start with a game or exercise designed to challenge individuals into revealing new or surprising information about themselves.

Practitioner's Enquiries

What would be an appropriate level of information for *you* to share with your colleagues?

What factors might influence that disclosure, and how as a trainer could you optimize those conditions for others?

What types of information would you want people to disclose in the context of this intervention?

What type of activity would best elicit the types of individual disclosure necessary for the team to grow?

What types of hidden knowledge would you want to be revealed in the context of this intervention?

What type of activity would best encourage this type of revelation?

What types of conditions and contexts could you apply to facilitate this process?

For instance, often people tend to reveal far more 'real' information about themselves when pressured or stressed. The addition of a tight deadline and real ramifications for task success or failure can, combined with an effective process review, illuminate far more than the same task with no consequence or time pressure.

The cooperation of the two retinas in one field of vision, whatever is its cause, must rather be the source of all the ideas to which single or double vision may give rise.

Johannes P. Muller (Physiologist)

FROM INDIVIDUAL TO GROUP, AND GROUP TO TEAM

As individuals aggregate, certain things happen in terms of their interpersonal dynamics. A tool that can be helpful in demystifying this process is Bruce Tuckman's Four Stages of Team Development (1965) which was developed in the mid-1960s (see Figure 3.2). The model presents a description of the journey a team might make as they work together over a period of time. As the team matures, the nature of the relationship between them will change as will, where relevant, the relationship between a team and its leader.

Forming

As a group of individuals comes together, those individuals will typically be very dependent on a leader – whether formal or informal – for guidance. There can be little debate, disagreement or discussion regarding anything more than the actual task at hand. They will often be very polite to each other and tolerance will be gently tested. Based on the three conditions for effective teamwork, as stated above, it could be argued that this collective is not yet a team, but a group with the same job – like a bunch of strangers running to catch the same bus.

Practitioner's Enquiries

What needs to precede any learning exercise in order for groups to engage with it in an optimal way? (See Part I of this book for more about this.)

How 'easy' or 'difficult' a task would be helpful at this stage? Too difficult and the new group will be overawed with the scale of the undertaking, too easy and you risk the group not moving on to the next stage of the journey.

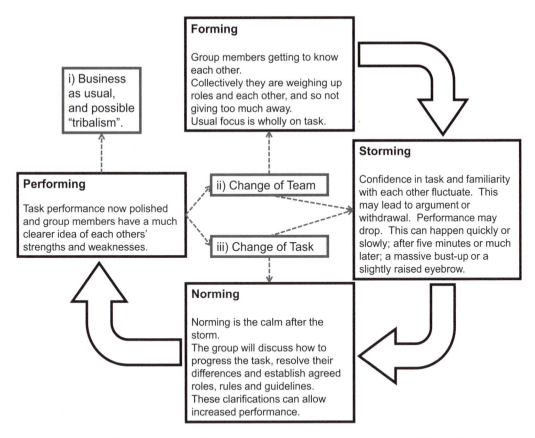

Figure 3.2   Tuckman's team formation model (with experiential learning adaptation)

Individual roles and responsibilities are yet to be ascertained and often people, particularly those who need roles to be defined, may be uncomfortable.

Storming

As things progress, members will often vie for position, challenging the roles and decisions of each other and more forcefully establishing team aims. This increase in strength of positional assertion may result in a 'storm' – a conflict, argument or full-blown row between individuals or factions. Although these storms are often explicitly concerned with the task at hand and the manner in which it should be approached, it is frequently the case that individuals' personal agendas or insecurities may be the root cause.

Because of this, although the focus is on the task, performance may drop as a result of the conflict and resultant ill-feeling.

Compromises may be necessary, within the team, at this point in order for progress to be enabled. It is surprising how tensions can rise even when the learning experience is artificial. Recently I overheard a pair of participants working on a task beginning to disagree on how it should be completed. As the intensity (and the volume) of the conversation increased to fever pitch, one partner suddenly started to laugh and said to the other, 'Dude! It's a fictional task!'

Often, keen to avoid discomfort and conflict in a group, inexperienced trainers and facilitators intervene when groups storm. However, this intervention can potentially do more harm than good, as it can inhibit full expression and progress and therefore learning.

Practitioner's Enquiries

What artificial pressures could you apply to a group to act as storm-catalysts?

Is this ethical, or should you simply let the team evolve at its own pace? Your answer here may be affected by the amount of time you have available for the total intervention, including learning review.

What factors impact upon how comfortable you (as facilitator) would be with a group conflicting in front of you? How far/long before you stepped in?

Given that the learning of the group is what is fundamental here, how can you detach yourself from any conflict and focus on what is really important?

In Tuckman's model, teams move from the storm into a clear state of effective business as usual (the 'norm'). However, this transition is far more likely to be a series of short and increasingly productive mini-squalls interspersed with effective workings. This process takes time and is not always obvious. Storming can be a full-blown row, but it can equally be a raised eyebrow. As facilitator, if you decide to base your theoretical underpinning for an exercise on this model, you need to notice a huge range of signals and discern when a gesture or discourse is pivotal.

Norming

If the group passes through these storms, they will frequently form stronger agreements and consensuses. Bigger decisions may be made as a whole group; smaller ones potentially delegated to a sub-group. Individual roles and contributions may be more recognized and acknowledged within the progress towards any agreed and shared goals. Communication has become more honest and probably therefore effective. Community is very strong at this point and the group may well start to socialize together.

Of course, in reality, groups sometimes *must* pass through the storms into something vaguely effective for the sake of a task that takes priority. Their salary depends on it. However, in the artifice of a training room, a storm can sometimes be effectively the end of any productive learning. As a facilitator, you will need to handle these situations carefully and review the conflict skilfully in order to avoid this breakdown.

> **Practitioner's Enquiries**
>
> What behaviours might a 'normed' and effective team be exhibiting?
>
> Could you raise this hypothetically with a team before an activity in order to provide a comparator in a post-exercise review?
>
> If working with an established (or 'normed') team, what types of challenges and pressures would facilitate their improvement from good to excellent?

Performing

The final of Tuckman's stages is represented by a team which is strategically aware and is taking responsibility for its own actions and direction by making shared values-based decisions against agreed criteria. Disagreements can occur and they are quickly resolved through positive discussion. Performance is optimized as the team focuses on the task and looks after its members in appropriate balance.

The journey from 'form' to 'perform' can take differing lengths of time dependent on a number of factors. However, it is unlikely to occur with only one or two task experiences. It is also the case that any change, whether it be a new type of task or a change in team personnel, can result in revisiting any of the earlier stages.

This cyclical journey will often result in learning. If you present a long, complex exercise, it is possible that a group may experience one cycle, and learn a little. If, however, you present a series of well-constructed, short exercises that each build on the previous one, and each experience is reviewed effectively, then you may achieve far greater progress in the same amount of time as the group will experience multiple cycles.

> **Practitioner's Enquiries**
>
> How likely is it that a team will reach 'performing' in your session?
>
> In the time allocated, how many learning cycles are viable?
>
> What can you do as a facilitator to maximize this number?

Eventually, it may be the case that, when a team has consistently performed well, the integrity and importance of the team identity takes on paramount importance. This so-called tribalism can actually result in *decreased* performance as individuals become unwilling to challenge the process or disrupt the balance of relationships. As a facilitator, it may become necessary for you to intervene if you notice this occurring. Healthy teams should be receptive to challenge from inside and out – this is what keeps them performing.

In Chapter 4, we will look at John Adair's model for functional leadership. As leaders can only lead when there are followers to be led, the model is useful for teamwork development as well. In fact, as you read Chapters 3 and 4, you will notice that all teamwork theory and exercises can be used for leadership development and vice versa: the difference is in the set-up and, crucially, in the review of the activities.

Here, for convenience, is a slightly adapted version of Adair's circles (Figure 3.3):

Figure 3.3   Adair's intersecting circles adapted to illustrate team balance

Without a task, there would be no function for a team and it is also this which often takes the whole of a team's attention – sometimes appropriately, of course. Other times, such as in a training session, it is less appropriate to be disproportionately concerned with the task.

The needs of the team, including the way the team communicates and functions together, must be attended to if the group is going to progress beyond being a collection of individuals working near each other.

A team is, of course, made up of individuals, all of which come to the group with their individual experience, enthusiasms and needs. An effective team is aware of these and will assist and support each individual as appropriate.

Practitioner's Enquiries

In your exercise designs, what would be the particular needs of the task itself? What jobs would need to be completed in order for a successful outcome to be reached?

What specifically would a team be doing that a group of disparate individuals would not?

What individual motivations, preferences and agendas might need to be managed by you (or by the team) in order for success to occur?

This three-fold model is so simple that many participants will adopt it easily as a framework for both planning and reviewing activities. A conversation at the start of an activity which checks that all the information and resources for the task are available, that everyone is clear both on what is required of them as a team and on how the team is going to approach the task, and then takes note of any individual queries, contributions or problems is a great way to begin. Likewise, at the end of an activity, being able to discuss (sometimes very quickly) how successfully the task was executed, how well the team worked together and to clear up any individual matters will help a team enormously to grow together in function and communication and will encourage individuals to reach their own potential.

Of course remember that a *task* 'success' can lead to the feeling that the *team* worked and that every *individual* was replete and happy. Similarly a task failure can disguise all manner of positive team and individual successes. Neither position is necessarily an accurate reflection of truth, and so it is essential that you as facilitator remain focused on the process even if everyone is firmly fixed on the task-oriented goal.

> *Thought and theory must precede all salutary action; yet action is nobler in itself than either thought or theory.*
>
> Virginia Woolf (Author)

There are many further tools which are useful, in the hands of skilled practitioners, in discerning individuals' contributions to teamwork. The ones we have found to be particularly useful in this setting are

- Strength Deployment Inventory[1]
- Belbin® Team Roles[2]
- Myers Briggs Type Indicator[3]

All of these tools are tools are simple and straightforward if taken at face value and the insights they offer are valuable. However, as a caveat to the reader, all three are protected by various levels of copyright and all require training and accreditation to be fully utilized. As such, we wholeheartedly recommend you understand the theory and concepts behind the tool, use this thinking first and foremost, and if you want to use the tool itself you invest in the appropriate training and qualifications.

Integrating Theory with Activity – Developing the Core Attributes of Teamwork

As mentioned above, 'teamwork' is built around three core aspects. When considering new activities for developing these aspects, it is important to have an idea at the start of which of these would be useful to focus on.

For example, let's say that you want to focus on building trust between team members. I can think of several occasions when I have been working with a person I do not trust – either personally or professionally. Regardless of the multitude of procedures and

---

1   See: http://uk.personalstrengths.com.

2   See: http://www.belbin.com.

3   See: http://www.mbti.com.

processes that are employed to optimize communication or to ensure that different team members' strengths are deployed effectively, if I do not trust the people I am working with then I will always hold back. Now, if my trust has been lost due to a specific incident, then this will need to be addressed directly and all the training-room activities in the world will not help. However, it is more common that my trust has simply not yet been earned, and this can be developed efficiently through artificial experiential learning.

You must trust and believe in people or life becomes impossible.

Anton Chekov (Playwright)

So, to illustrate the creative process, here are a few quickly conceived trust-building experiential activities. To provide a quick taste of the types of activities you may come up with, we've applied a 3x3 formula of invention.

Three situations where trust-building might be necessary are thus:[4]

Building Trust Within a Team	An embryonic team who don't know each other well
	A team who rely on each other to protect their physical wellbeing and safety
	A situation where certain work packages must be delegated and performed separately, without opportunity for wholesale checking and mutual control

For each of these three situations, we came up with three ideas for activities, as shown below.

		Other attributes that might be elicited by this exercise
Situation One A learning task for a new team that don't know each other well	**Example Exercise One** Take a random collection of objects (coat hanger, pipe-cleaner, string, child's stickers…) or holiday postcards and ask each member to choose one that illustrates how they feel about their part in this group. Invite other members to respond.	Disclosure Listening Giving and receiving feedback
	Example Exercise Two Ask the team to plan a trip from the current location to Casablanca using as many different modes of transport as there are team members. Each member to be assigned a method of transport, with justification.	Discerning impact on others Creativity Self-disclosure

4   Normally, such scenarios are enacted in a controlled, regulated and qualified high-ropes or equivalent environment. We're not suggesting a replacement, but something that might pre-empt any more physically challenging experience.

Situation One continued	**Example Exercise Three** Provide a large range of objects, each with a discernable (and not universally stigmatized) smell (citrus fruit, flowers, leather, unprocessed wool, strong cheese, perfume...). Each team member to be assigned a smell, based on first impression, with justification.	Discerning impact on others Individual contributions Giving and receiving feedback
Situation Two A learning task for a team who (may) rely on each other to protect their physical wellbeing and safety *These exercises all involve the use of blindfolds. This is simply because, deprived of sight, people will frequently feel as if their physical wellbeing is at stake when actually they are perfectly safe. When using blindfolds for learning experiences, do be aware of the emotional wellbeing of participants, who may occasionally panic.*	**Example Exercise Four** Closely surrounded by the rest of the team, each member in turn must balance blindfolded on a low object (inverted bucket? sturdy stool? chair?), stand one-legged, stretch the other straight out in front of them and then touch both sets of toes with both hands.	Self-disclosure Communication
	Example Exercise Five Over lunch, blindfold half the team and forbid the sighted half from using their hands. The sighted team members must then instruct the others in how to feed themselves. Then swap over. Alternatives could include dressing in safety gear, making a jam sandwich, basic first aid, painting a self-portrait and so on.	Communication Equality and diversity awareness Clear instruction and feedback
	Example Exercise Six While blindfolded, the team must be directed around an obstacle course, without being touched, by one sighted leader who is standing at the end of the course. Obstacles could include things to go around, under, over or even through.	Communication Equality and diversity awareness Clear instruction and feedback
Situation Three Where certain work packages must be delegated and performed separately, without opportunity for wholesale checking and mutual control	**Example Exercise Seven** Show the group a famous picture, then give each group member a piece of blank paper. Ask them to produce a team representation of the famous picture, by each creating a 'piece of the jigsaw'. Allow five minutes to plan, then five minutes silent and isolated execution of the creation. Then recombine pieces and review the result.	Planning Delegation Flexibility
	Example Exercise Eight Split the team into three or four sub-groups. Each are given a brief to create a defined portion of (for example) a pantomime cow. Give five minutes collective planning, then separate the sub-teams. Give 15 minutes for portion construction and three minutes for collective assembly.	Planning Goal-setting Flexibility

	Example Exercise Nine	
Situation Three continued	Select a poem which is of an appropriate length (200–300 words?). Give the team two minutes to plan and then five minutes, during which they must separate. The whole poem must be recited from memory at the end of the five minutes. Each team member must contribute equally; and there should be a penalty for a team unable to do this perfectly. Adapt the timings dependent on the length of the poem relative to the size of the team.	Strategizing Stress management Individual contributions

The ideas above will all work given some context and input from you regarding the precise details. However, below is a fully worked-through exercise that will work as it is.

Getting Teams Working Exercise: 'Editorial'

The aim of this activity is to bring team communication, roles and task organization into focus in a time-sensitive environment. It would be suitable for a large number of people, down to a minimum of eight people in two groups of four.

Brief

(Option 1) Create a four-page newspaper with original material, using the equipment provided.

Or

(Option 2) Create a four-page newspaper with original material, using the equipment provided, including stories, pictures, a cartoon, puzzle and letters page. Stories should be true and based around the recent experience of the group members.

Time allowed: 45 minutes.

Materials (for each group of four to five)

Option 1	**Option 2**
eight sheets of A3 paper	laptop
pens	printing and copying facilities
rulers	digital camera
pencils	paper and pens

LEARNING REVIEW FOR EDITORIAL ACTIVITY

A learning review for this task could be focused in different ways: task organization; communication; team roles.

Below are some questions to help in reviewing this task.

What was great about the way you worked together in that task?

What could you have done differently to work more effectively?

How was the work divided out?

How did you decide on the content of the paper?

Was everyone happy with the content decided upon? How do you know?

Who had most of the ideas?

Who was the leader? How was this decided?

How did the timing go?

Where is the plan for the layout? Who created this?

How did you feel during the task?

On a rating scale of 1–10, where 10 = you did everything and 1 = you did nothing, how involved were you in this task?

How important was what you did to the overall success of the task?

When I have run this exercise, a leader is usually quick to emerge, using one of a range of different styles and with varying degrees of success. When you work with teams, the impact of the leader, whether that is a formal or informal role, quickly comes to the fore as a criterion for the success or otherwise of a team's function. The facilitation of leadership as a separate issue will be explored fully in the next chapter.

4 *Facilitating Leadership Development*

Leadership is the art of getting someone else to do something you want done because he wants to do it.
> Dwight Eisenhower (Military Commander and US President)

This chapter is not about leadership per se. There are many great books on leadership already and many of them deal extensively with what leadership is and is not. For us, leadership can be many things. We write and run our leadership exercises to reveal and explore the following facets: vision, values, influence, flexibility, motivation, supporting others and gaining their support, behaving with personal authenticity and clear communication to the team of all of the above. The development of leadership potential is clearly more than this tokenistic list, but this gives a flavour of the ethos with which we approach our learning designs.

Leadership development interventions can be very challenging, not least because everyone present probably feels that they should be leading, or may feel that *their* way is the right way. As Jo Owen says in *How to Lead* (2005), 'It is not easy to lead leaders.' This tension can make for powerful learning if it is acknowledged and reviewed appropriately. After all it is rare that, as professionals, we get to experience someone else at work and be free to simply watch and learn.

Any of the exercises in this book can be used to provide a leadership focus. The key difference if you are wanting to develop leaders is that the focus of the review must be purely on the leadership shown, and not just on the overall performance. In this chapter we provide a consideration of the issues of how else experiential learning can serve leadership development, an examination of some of the problems that need to be addressed if it is to be done well, and a sample exercise that illustrates how simple kit can provide powerful lessons.

For this book and to provide a more widely-known context, a framework that we've found useful to capture the essence of what leaders *do* is Kouzes and Posner's *Leadership Challenge* model (2007). In this work they propose that, 'Leadership is not about personality; it's about behaviour,' which is perfectly aligned to experiential development activity where people are required to *do* things and then talk about them. Kousez and Posner judge that effective leaders exhibit five main types of behaviour.

Behaviour Type 1: Modelling the Way

Leading by example, with a clear sense of authentic values. Ensuring that team actions are aligned with the shared values.

Values offer huge territory for experiential learning, as even the simplest of tasks can be carried out to certain standards. In a training room, the 'standard' will often be determined by a team or group, seemingly without intervention from a formal leader. However, one group member will *always* have made a formal decision, which is then followed by another member. Hence, leadership through example and values.

Behaviour Type 2: Inspiring a Shared Vision

Creating a future vision of success and enlisting others in a common vision by appealing to shared aspirations.

Vision and imagination again offer a range of options for experiential learning. A blank sheet of paper, some marker pens and a creative brief will allow certain individuals the space to start asking questions of their team about how a solution might be realized and which options would suit the team members.

Behaviour Type 3: Challenging the Process

Searching for opportunities by looking outward for innovative solutions. Taking risks and learning from these experiences to continually learn and improve.

Again, even the simplest of games can be made very powerful by the addition of a few 'rules'. It is often the case that the task rules (what to do) will be followed completely; while the procedural and team rules (how to do it and how to behave) will sometimes be broken with abandon. This is 'challenging the process' and again is very easy to simulate in a training environment. However, as John Adair says in *How to Grow Leaders* (2005), 'To act is easy, to think hard.' So much of the value of experiential leadership situations comes from a strong facilitated review of what has just happened, and more importantly *why* it just happened.

Behaviour Type 4: Enable Others to Act

Fostering teams and cooperative bodies by building trust and facilitating relationships. Developing individual's competencies by encouraging self-confidence and initiative.

The most basic of team tasks can be led in a huge variety of ways, from complete empowerment of team to extreme micro-management. Feedback on the degree of control and influence that a leader has at any given point can be hugely illuminating, and facilitating this feedback is a key part of leadership development success.

Behaviour Type 5: Encourage the Heart

Creating a spirit of community, through the recognition of individual contributions and by showing appreciation of excellence.

The addition of a feedback component can raise even the simplest 'game' to something very powerful for all concerned if it is focused on the leader's words, their tone and on their individual and specific behaviours. Also, the potential for short-term successes and failures of a team can give great scope for noting how different leaders praise and celebrate good performance; how they deal with setbacks, and whether they take opportunities to continually improve – regardless of artificial success or failure.

Leaders Need Followers

Experiential leadership training is difficult to do with one person at a time. This is not to discount the value of coaching, mentoring or facilitated review of a real-life experience. However, in the artificial construct of the training room or high-ropes course, we're assuming here that the experiential learning environment comprises a situation where between four and ten people come together to learn about leadership with a facilitator.

Another advantage of the home-made activity and approach is that it can far more easily adapt to departures from the ideal. Several years ago, I spent a hugely frustrating day on a course where the trainer was using a very expensive and convoluted case study which was written for a team of *six* people. Hypothetically, this was a great exercise, but was ill-suited for the *seven* trainees in our group. I spent hours being an 'observer' (with no instruction with regard to what I should be looking for) and then, with the 'leadership' task completed we moved on to another task. The glossiness of the product prevented flexibility by the trainer, and the experience dominated any review of the learning. However, I learned an important lesson that day: namely, to always write at least two extra (but seamlessly removable) roles, parts or options into any given exercise in case you're presented with odd group sizes.

If you are in the business of developing leaders then you have to grasp the difficult fact that leaders need followers. This sounds like a truism, but it is very difficult to experientially develop leadership in ten people at the same time. Any member present can learn vicariously, or by focused observation, or by providing feedback to a leader, but it's unlikely (nay impossible) that every group member will be able to lead simultaneously. Without a little focus at the start, many of the myriad opportunities offered for leadership development by experiential learning can be wasted. Usually what transpires is that the team is set a challenge by the trainer, they succeed or fail and any extracted learning is usually shared by the team out of collective responsibility.

This is not necessarily a problem if the trainer's intent is to build a team; but it does represent an opportunity wasted if the learning intent was intended to be around individual leadership. To move a teamwork activity into a leadership activity requires a little thought and focus from the trainer.

Practitioner's Enquiries

In any given exercise will it be obvious who is leading?

Will this be designated by the group or by you?

Will the leader be chosen before the task is outlined or in the planning process? (Both have benefits, but the former usually promotes more powerful learning as it probably requires an individual to lead from a place of discomfort.)

If an 'official' leader is chosen, is it obvious what everyone else should be doing?

Do you have time (over the course of the entire intervention, not just this exercise) for everyone to take a leadership role? Does everyone know this?

Will there be time for proper feedback from the team to the leader and vice versa?

Have you set the climate of the group correctly so that feedback can be offered supportively and without fear of reprisal at a later point?

'We Didn't Have a Leader. We Just Got on and Did it...'

Many experiential leadership learning tasks (build a tower, cross a river, carry a ball and so on) can be completed successfully if the group cooperate and efficiently 'muddle through'. Team leadership sometimes rotates very flexibly from minute to minute, especially in a training-room environment where normal line-management hierarchies have been removed. This fluidity is normally labelled as 'teamwork'. From second to second, leaders will emerge and disappear according to need. This is no bad thing – and certainly not to be discouraged. However, at the end of the exercise, the group can be left with a feeling that, 'We just got on and did it,' or 'We just *made* that decision'. Without a quality review this type of thinking isn't particularly helpful, because it misses the point that an individual made a decision and chose a course of action. The concept that each member of a team came, individually, to exactly the same decision at the same moment and telepathically passed this instantaneously to the rest of the group is highly unlikely. More probable is that someone took a decision (leader), and the rest of the group (followers) went along with it. In groups, decisions don't 'just happen'.

What is crucial here is that often when groups don't nominate a leader or when someone is not obviously in charge they can feel that there was no leader at all. It is essential then, that any exercise is followed by a clear review designed to challenge this type of thinking, and so then allow individuals who did lead, influence, challenge the process and so on, to have their actions recognized and reaffirmed so they can recreate them in different circumstances.

It is also important when you design a leadership exercise to consider how you could artificially empower a leader or allow the group to pause and think who might lead, how they might lead, and how the group might want to be led.

Suggested Strategies

Before any task starts, offer the group a number of role choices: this can be a written brief or verbal, and may contain this type of information:

In the next exercise, you must take a specific role. These roles are:

Leader

Team Manager

Task Manager

Resources Controller

…and whatever else might suit the task. (You can have one role per participant, or leave some members without pre-designated functions.)

Decide on these roles, let me know, and then you will be handed the task brief. You must make your decision in the next two minutes.

Such a brief will prime the post-task review and will start to get the group to explore roles with more clarity. I sat through a seminar once where the teacher lectured for over an hour about the theoretical differences between leadership and management. The same learning could have been delivered in a fraction of the time by giving a task and allowing the team to choose a 'leader' and 'manager'; as this would immediately promote a conversation about what the difference between those two roles actually is.

Another, more prescriptive way of getting at the same learning would be simply to hand out the team roles yourself, but there is always then the risk of participants suspecting an agenda on your part (for instance, 'You chose Jon to lead because you knew we'd fall out…' or 'Yeah, but Sue was the natural manager anyway').

A strategy to avoid this is simple leadership and other role rotation. This is somewhat predictable and allows participants to switch off when they know it won't be their turn. Over time, we've found it far more effective to introduce a note of serendipity into the proceedings.

For example, prepare some individual instructions, one per participant. Cut them up, fold them so the information is hidden, and allow the group to choose one each. The information may say things like:

You are the leader. In the next exercise it is your job to lead.
Even if you don't have the requisite knowledge of the task, you are in charge and the others will look to you for leadership.

On the next task, there is a leader. But it isn't you.

You are the loyal supporter. Someone in the group will emerge as leader.
Don't overtly reveal your loyalty but you must support your leader 100 per cent.

You are the embittered cynic. Regardless of your personal feelings
it is your job to challenge the leadership shown on this next exercise.

Forcing the leadership issue in this way also has the advantage of separating out task affinity and actual transferable leadership ability. I once manned a teamwork exercise on an outdoor activity circuit which involved scaffold construction. Several teams came to the exercise over the course of a day's training circuit. And in *every* case the males took the tools, gloves and poles and left the females to watch the clock and calculate the cost of resources used. The men had no idea what they were doing, but they grabbed for the tools quicker and so roles became entrenched. What is interesting is that the women didn't challenge this until after the exercise was completed. They simply let the boys have their toys because it avoided confrontation and then everyone could go home more quickly.

Often leadership exercises are like this, as the group member who understands the task, or who shouts the loudest, becomes the leader. Because of the artifice of the situation, it sometimes needs a little manipulation to ensure that everyone gets chance to experience the hot seat.

Extreme volume in music very often disguises a lack of actually important content.

Michael Tilson Thomas (Conductor)

This issue becomes massively amplified if the same group of learners are going to be put together for a longer period of time (such as a company management development programme or residential course). This is why the design of any intervention and an appropriate learning review *at the end of each task* is even more important.

Task, Process or Individual Leadership

Building from the possibility that an individual can lead simply because they understand a task more readily, it is worth considering what type of leadership your exercise and observations are appropriate to capture. For instance, it is entirely possible for an individual to lead a group to a solved puzzle without engaging at all with the individuals in the group or the team as a collective entity. John Adair's *Functional Leadership* writings and model can provide a helpful framework to build on here.[1] Adair's model essentially states that effective leaders get to grips with the needs of the task, the team and the individuals within it. The differences between these three are clear in spite of the overlap between them.

---

1   See *Leadership and Motivation* for a good overview of Adair's model (Adair, 2006).

Task	Right, you, put tab X into slot Y.
Team	Does everyone understand what's going on?
Individual	Bob, are you OK?

All are necessary for long-term successful leadership, but in a short, artificial training world the 'team' and 'individual' elements can be omitted and the task still 'successfully' completed. Since the task was completed participants can argue that this type of leadership works; which is conveniently blind to the unreality of the context. The flip-side of this is that back in reality leaders do often have authority because they understand the needs of the task. As such, careful management of the learning experience and review is required.

Adair's work is adapted for an experiential learning environment below:

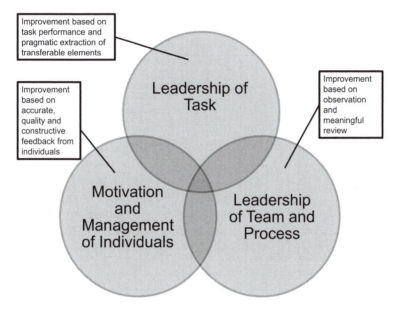

Figure 4.1   Adair's functional leadership model with experiential learning annotation

If a leader is to learn and develop (especially in an artificial setting) they need three main things:

- First, to be able to extract transferable lessons about the leadership of that specific type of task.
- Second, to have clear data (from a variety of sources) about how they handled the team and the process behind the task.
- Third, to have real, meaningful, well-delivered constructive feedback from the individuals in question.

Again, all these factors need to be built into to your exercise and debrief designs.

Practitioner's Enquiries

Does your leadership exercise replicate the *type* of task that an individual might experience in their daily life?

If so, will the exercise offer the right level of challenge (and how could you make it more complex or simple, quickly and easily)?

If not, how might the team and people processes be a reflection of reality?

What opportunities could you design in for leading different types of individuals?

Will your exercise need everyone in the team to work or can it be conquered by one person and five spectators?

Will the information that you provide to the leader be different to that which you give to the rest of the group?

Could you give the leader extra time to familiarize themselves with the brief, so as to create an authority with regard to the task?

Developing the Core Attributes of Leadership

If your intention is to develop leadership potential of individuals, then on top of these considerations, you'll need to consider the focus of the leader as well as simply what the team is supposed to be doing. This is usually far more possible with an exercise designed from scratch and often prohibited by store-bought training experiences.

In order to do this, you need to ask yourself what, personally, do you believe leadership to be?

Practitioner's Exercise

List the top seven *behaviours* that you believe effective leaders exhibit. Be careful that you are focusing on demonstrable behaviours, not nebulous attributes.

For each of these seven, think of three situations that you could offer an opportunity for a learner to display that behaviour.

For each of those three, apply the objective-led exercise design principles from Chapter 1. Repeat three times. Consider what other leadership attributes would be accessed by your exercise.

For example, as a worked example, let's say that effective leaders 'articulate a clear vision of a successful outcome'. Since, as John P. Kotter says in *Leading Change* (1996), effective leadership is about dealing with change, and change in turn requires a clearly articulated vision of destination.

Vision is central to leadership. Most store-bought leadership experiences have a clear answer, and many require no real artistic, business or intellectual imagination to complete or achieve a viable solution; yet leaders often need help in both formulating a vision of where they want to go, persuading themselves and others that it is a vision worth following, and then clearly articulating it to their staff or followers.

You can't blow an uncertain trumpet.

Theodore Hesburgh (Theologian and Educator)

So, when we went through the process above, off the top of our heads these were the first three learning situations we considered. They are not necessarily wholly accurate – this piece is included simply to demonstrate the developmental thought process at work.

Articulation of clear vision of successful outcome	**1) Situation One** A learning task with a brief that is completely open and requires imagination and courage to strive for.
	2) Situation Two A learning task where the 'answer' is given to the leader, but not to the followers.
	3) Situation Three A learning task where the solution runs contrary to the needs of the group (for example, localized hardship such as having to work through a lunch-break).

Building on this, here are nine (three by three) off-the-cuff exercises that would go some way towards accessing those characteristics.

		Other attributes that might be elicited by this exercise
Situation One A learning task with a brief that is completely open and requires imagination and courage to strive for.	**Example Exercise One** Provide a box of art materials, old magazines and wall-lining paper and have them lead a group in the planning, creation and execution of a mural to represent what their organization stands for.	Discussion and agreement on key team values. Motivating different types of people to be creative.
	Example Exercise Two Provide them with a box of random objects and task them with leading the group in using the objects to produce a genuinely saleable product or service. Then have them go out and sell it to the public.	Planning. Creativity. Critical thinking. Commercial awareness.
	Example Exercise Three Provide the leader with an amount of cash (to be returned) and have them lead the group in collectively choosing a charity and maximizing the given money for the good cause.	Demonstration of clear and shared values. Motivating individuals. Creativity.

	Example Exercise Four Provide the leader with an obscure picture, give them three minutes to familiarize themselves with it, take it away from them, and then give them 15 minutes to instruct their team in the recreation of the image using household rubbish as sculpture materials.	Creativity. Motivation. Values. Communication.
Situation Two A learning task where the 'answer' is given to the leader, but not to the followers.	Example Exercise Five Provide the leader with the coordinates of a destination. Then give them ten minutes to lead their team in creating a map from their current position to the given location, using a compass, ruler, coloured pencils and paper.	Clear communication. Creativity. Defining the parameters of the objective (who is the map *for*?)
	Example Exercise Six Have the leader lead the group in rearranging the furniture and moveable fittings in the room to create their own (that is, the leader's) ideal working environment. Allow 20 minutes for the planning and execution of this task.	Clear vision and communication. Effective assigning of tasks to appropriate team members. Time management.
	Example Exercise Seven Give the group ten minutes to inventory a stock cupboard or a large biscuit-tin full of old screws and other ironmongery.	Motivation. Task assignment. Time management.
Situation Three A learning task where the solution runs contrary to the needs of the group (for example, localized hardship such as having to work through a lunch-break).	Example Exercise Eight Set a task which, to be completed successfully, requires the group to work together 'out of hours'. For instance, at the end of a session, give the team a short story and require them to dramatize and rehearse it and arrive ready to perform at the next formal training session.	Creativity. Managing performance. Managing work/life commitments.
	Example Exercise Nine Provide the leader with a set of instructions for tasks to assign, some of which require the assigned team member to work in a physically separate location for all or some of the task. For instance, a treasure hunt with items on the list that necessitate the group dividing to collect them.	Team roles. Coordination. Planning.

Again, not all of these would necessarily work – although all have potential. The issue here is that with some clear thought into the learning intent it is possible to create powerful leadership experiences which (with sensible set-up and a good quality review) will give developing leaders a potentially hugely powerful experience upon which any theoretical or later real-life experience can sit. And remember that these samples were created simply by using 'vision' as a starting block. Building from this process, it is possible to start combining different facets of leadership into exercise design. Rather than prescribe more, we simply pose the types of questions that would be helpful in designing powerful experiences around leadership development.

VISION

We don't know where you're going, so how can we know the way?

St Thomas (Apostle)

Leading, by its very nature, involves movement. Movement, if it is to have purpose, is towards a goal and it is the vision, or knowledge, of the goal that provides direction for those being led. A great leader will have an assured vision of what is to be achieved, and it is often this which will inspire people to follow.

Of course, the vision must also be clearly communicated to those following. The trainer or facilitator can focus on either or both of these aspects of vision in an experiential setting.

Practitioner's Enquiries

Where will the focus of the exercise be? Is it possible to complete the task without a clear leadership oversight?

Is the leader required merely to manage resources, or actually make leadership judgements about the destination of the task?

How willing are you to allow the frameworks of your learning activity to be challenged by a group? What is acceptable vision-based creative challenge, and what will destroy the integrity of the experience?

VALUES

We all have a set of values which we live by – those standards which we will fight for, those which we use as a basis for decisions, those which, when our life reflects them, result in us feeling fulfilled. Effective leaders will have a certain knowledge of what their values are and are prepared to communicate those values to the rest of the team. They are also able to balance these values against each other so that each decision they make, whether planned or apparently impulsive, is in line with what they judge to be the most important value at the time.

Management is doing things right, leadership is doing the right thing.

Peter F. Drucker (Writer and Consultant)

For instance, if we say that a leader in a workplace values real quality of production and the self-confidence of their team members. When a team member receives a valid complaint from a client and is upset, the leader makes a choice as to what is most important at the time – the team member or the valid complaint. How the leader behaves in this situation will have a huge impact on the team member, but is a decision ultimately based on the leader's value system.

Practitioner's Enquiries

Can you see potential opportunities for decisions to be made that involve standards and qualities (as well as different routes to the same end point)?

Are there any ramifications if a group's standards are not up to scratch? Can quality control become an issue?

Could you include rules that are 'breakable' and still achieve a viable task result? Often rules related to task are treated as immutable, but rules related to process or individual behaviour are more fluid, though there is technically no reason why a group should behave in this way. Rule-breaking opens up interesting values-based avenues of review discussion.

Could you introduce penalties if certain parts of the brief are not adhered to?

Could you ask the leader to allocate a fixed amount of resource between causes of differing worth?

Can you factor into the design of the exercise choices whereby the leader has to set team harmony against successful task?

If a leadership development intervention is to be of any value whatsoever it has to allow a leader to make choices based on values. The great thing is that all decisions have some sort of value system behind them, and a good learning review will acknowledge and unpack that.

DECISION-MAKING

Building on from vision and values, the capacity to make and take responsibility for decisions is a key facet of effective leadership. This is especially true when an important decision needs to be made under pressure. Whether the leader takes the 'right' path based on logic and rational analysis, or the 'best' path based on intuition, is less important than the leader having the courage to stand by their convictions. However, both aspects of decision-making offer interesting territory for feedback and review.

INFLUENCING AND MOTIVATING INDIVIDUALS

Coaches who can outline plays on a black board are a dime a dozen. The ones who win get inside their players and motivate.

Vince Lombardi (American football coach)

Practitioner's Enquiries

Is there any way to hold the leader to account for the decisions that the team collectively take (as would be the case in reality)?

Can you think of a way to add personal reward to a leader if their team performs to a certain standard?

Can you manipulate the time that a decision has to be made in?

Can you alter the amount of briefing information, so that it is revealed at certain points, thus affecting the leader's strategic planning?

Can you alter the rules of engagement mid-way through a case study or exercise? (A printout of an 'email from the CEO' with the new rules on is a quick way of doing this.)

Is there scope for discussion around your activity for whether the 'best' or the 'right' path was taken at any given point? Which path would *you* have taken?

All the vision, values and decision-making powers in the world will only get a leader so far. If they are unable to use these to motivate the people who are following them, their efforts will be futile.

The difference between authentically leading and having a badge which says 'In Charge' will often be the ability to understand that people are different and will be motivated by different approaches. The effective leader will be sufficiently flexible to speak to the motivation of each member of the team in order to ensure that they will follow because they want to, rather than because the boss has told them to.

Practitioner's Enquiries

Do you actually need to consider this issue at all in activity design? After all, it could be argued that leaders need to motivate others regardless of task.

What scope is there in the exercise to allow a leader to make decisions about whether to micro-manage or to trust and empower the team?

Could you leave the level of challenge or difficulty open to interpretation by the leader and thus allow them to stretch the limits of their motivational capability?

What motivational measures are you looking for? How will you (or the rest of the group) measure the leader's success as a motivator?

How ethical is it to put people in a position where motivation is difficult? Because it is a course people will be more tolerant than usual so conditions would need to be extreme for them to really struggle with motivation.

Allowing time at the beginning of a leadership-based intervention for participants to share a little of what is important to them will allow shrewd leaders to file that information away for when it is useful.

Imagine the impact when a participant speaks about their children early in a session; and an hour later in the middle of an exercise when looking for creative solutions, the leader says, 'X, what would your children make of this?' It may be that the children are particularly curious and the answer could provide helpful insight, or it may not be. Either way, the participant knows that the leader has listened to what has been said and is likely to feel valued and motivated as a result.

Leadership Exercise – Production Line

How many people: A team leader and a team (leader plus four to eight others is ideal).

Kit required:

A stack of plastic drinking cups.

An abundance of four different types of rubber bands. These need to be different lengths and strengths, not simply colour. Different sized paperclips, different sorts of children's beads, building blocks, or even types of dried pasta could also work well here.

Blindfolds (one per team member excluding the leader).

A stopwatch or clock.

Duration: Five to ten minutes activity plus review.

The objective: The leader to maximize performance of the team, as measured by production of completed delivery units.

The set-up: Nominate (or have the group nominate) on a leader. Take them outside and show them the four types of rubber band, and what one 'delivery unit' should look like. This consists of one cup, which contains just *one* of *each type* of rubber band (that is, one and only one of *each* type). To be really clear here, a completed unit is a cup with four different bands in it.

Prepare two sticky note signs – 'Sorting Area' and 'Dispatch Area'. Place a stack of paper cups on a table in the 'sorting area' and then blindfold all but one of the participants. Place the 'dispatch area' sign on a table across the room. Then, next to the cups empty a jumbled pile of lots of the different rubber bands. The more individual items the better. (Personally I like to raid a stationery cupboard and borrow a box of each of the four types and just mix them.)

Bring the leader back in and read the following brief (twice) to all the team.

This is an auditory brief that I will read twice. Your time will start when I finish reading for the second time.

You work for a stationery supplier and there has been a terrible mix-up here at the sorting area of the distribution depot and all the stock has been intermixed. You and your co-workers have the demanding task of sorting your supplies. In front of your team there is a large pile of mixed rubber bands containing several different types. There is also a stack of cups.

As a team, you will have five minutes to complete as many delivery units as you can. Each delivery unit consists of one cup, which contains just ONE of EACH TYPE of rubber band. When completed, each delivery unit is to be placed away from the sorting area, in the dispatch area (point this out to the leader) so that it can be inspected.

Your sighted leader may not touch the stationery, cups, sorting area or dispatch area. In addition, your sighted leader may not touch any of you (and vice versa). This is called 'harassment' and is a very serious breach of the rules.

Failure to stick to the rules will result in all materials and orders dispatched thus far being re-set to their initial position.

You'll need to stop the clock after five minutes and potentially keep a tally of quantity of orders. If you run out of cups, keep score and empty them back into the main pile.

Additional ideas:

Set a target for the team to achieve. Fifty plus is possible in five minutes.

Run the exercise in competition between departments or groups.

Run it in parallel in a large room, to engender some competitive pace.

Introduce no-speaking rules on certain key blindfolded members.

Add in random objects (a small coin) to confuse processes.

Introduce a performance-related real bonus as an incentive. (More than 20 units wins puddings at lunchtime, or similar.)

Things to look out for:

Does the leader empower and trust, or try to micro-manage each stage of the process?

Does the leader establish a production line (sorting, checking, transportation to dispatch) or do they allow a more organic approach?

How does the leader manage differences in performance from one team member to another? (Often the introduction of blindfolds leads to an identical approach towards all members.)

How does the leader generate enthusiasm for this trivial task? How do they maintain interest and enthusiasm for the full-time allocation?

How does the group react to the blindfolding, and how does the leader handle that?

So, having considered some different aspects of leadership in an experiential learning environment, what follows is a complete exercise that addresses several of these. Also presented are a number of ideas for a productive learning review. Of course, since any of the exercises in this book can be suitable for leadership development (as they can all be led), so the questions that surround the exercise and the review strategies are wholly transferable.

This is a short, sharp activity that can be used as a simple energizer for the start of a leadership session. However, if reviewed effectively it can also make great points about micro-management, empowering leadership, delegation, team communication and effective listening. I must admit that this is not my original concept. I saw a version of it on a teambuilding day a long time ago and adapted it heavily to place the focus on the leader.

This style of exercise works well for a number of reasons. As an energizer it's a quick fun way to start a session. It's particularly effective if the formal or informal hierarchies are reversed (that is, the natural or management 'leader' is blindfolded). However, it is a great tool to allow you to unpack group communications and shared language. It can also be a glorious illustrator of how empowering a team can be much more effective than micro-management.

The best executive is the one who has sense enough to pick good men to do what he wants done, and self-restraint to keep from meddling with them while they do it.

Theodore Roosevelt (US President)

HOW TO REVIEW THIS TYPE OF ACTIVITY TO EXTRACT THE MAXIMUM LEARNING

Based on our experience, the review of this type of exercise depends on the stance taken by the task leader who will either empower their team and simply provide vision and quality control, or they will micro-manage every single step for each worker.

However, with no prior knowledge, once the blindfolds are removed, I would start by celebrating how many completed units are in the dispatch area. Participants need to have their efforts acknowledged before you move on from the details of the task itself.

A wide open, 'What was that all about then?' question is always a good place to start. In responding to a question like this, participants take responsibility for guiding the discussion (and thus, the learning) themselves. A particularly chatty group might need little more prompting than this. However, this is unusual in our experience, so some control of the review will need to be retained. I would ask the sighted leader for their comments on the performance of the blindfolded workers: What did they do well? What could have been done better? And then I would ask the workers how they felt about the task and about the leader? What was good? What could be improved? I would request specificity from participants in all discussions.

What is vital here is that the focus is taken away from you as a facilitator and placed firmly on to the leader and the led. Often, when the learning focus is turned from a group performance (as with team experiences) to that of the leader, there can be resistance – especially if the task was not well executed. Often leaders and teams can challenge an exercise because, 'It wasn't real.' As a trainer or coach it can be easy to become defensive here. However keep in mind two things:

First, *it was real, because it just happened.*

Second (because of the previous point), the issue is *really* about the authenticity being displayed by the leader. What they are really saying with their challenge is, 'I'd have done it differently if you hadn't been watching,' which is a very different proposition. I find this a difficult conversation to have sometimes, but if explored well the issues and reflection around authenticity of behaviour can be very powerful.[2]

To continue, this exercise could focus on any given aspect of leadership but I might then, for example, ask what success means in this task. Is it sheer number of correctly completed units? Or is adherence to the rules also a measure of success? Were any rules broken, and if so, why did the leader choose to break them? This particular conversation can act as a neat segue into leadership values.

For more review questions, ideas and tools, revisit Part II of this book. However, the bottom line, as with every review conversation, must be to help the learners to capture the lesson so that they can remember it and use it when things change or go wrong back in their place of work.

So much of leadership development work is about allowing the learners to understand and reflect on their own style of leadership; and before individuals can lead nations, organizations, teams or even one other person, they must authentically and effectively lead themselves. What makes individuals effective and how you could help to be more so is where we head next.

---

2   Rob Goffee and Gareth Jones' book *Why Should Anyone be Led By You?* (2006) is particularly enlightening on the notion of authentic leadership, and as such is thoroughly recommended.

5 *Building Personal Effectiveness*

If you can dream – and not make dreams your master;
If you can think – and not make thoughts your aim;
If you can meet with Triumph and Disaster
And treat those two imposters just the same...
...Yours is the Earth and everything that's in it.

Rudyard Kipling – 'If'

The training and development world is full of talk about personal effectiveness. A quick scan through the literature suggests that the concept as we recognize it has its roots in the goal-oriented behaviour classic *How to Win Friends and Influence People* (Carnegie, 2006), which was first published in the 1930s. But Kipling's poem, *If*, written in 1895 and first published 15 years later, expresses many of exactly the same concepts. By detailing a range of concrete behaviours, Kipling describes many of the qualities we as facilitators would often want to focus upon in personal effectiveness interventions:

Calm, clear-headedness, self-awareness, receptiveness to feedback, patience, integrity, vision, focus, resilience, courage, discretion, perseverance, flexibility, articulateness, respect, self-reliance, time management...

So how is it possible to create an experiential intervention designed to enable people to become such paragons? I have run many sessions under the 'personal effectiveness' banner, both alone and with colleagues, and my answer to this question is simple: you can't. It might be just as reasonable to create a session on 'becoming splendid'. A beguiling title perhaps, but an unrealistic ambition for an afternoon course.

What you can do, however, is to create experiential learning activities which will encourage the development of one or more of the elements of personal effectiveness. Compared with much of the rest of the material in this book, the notion of personal effectiveness can be difficult to access in a multi-person setting. This is why many trainers (both of us included) are qualified coaches as well. However, a team experience can provide parallels with personal effectiveness if the task is suitably constructed. This chapter will explore several of the most relevant personal effective issues targets and suggest some ways that these can be developed in an artificial learning environment; whether as a personal enquiry, using group effectiveness as a metaphor or by observing individuals in a group setting.

Why is *Personal* Effectiveness Important to an Organization?

Most people recognize that they as individuals could function more effectively if they invested some reflection on their personal goals, motivations and habits. However, when goals and interim targets have been established at an organizational level, why would the leaders of that organization pay attention to the motivations and resultant habits of their employees? Surely it is sufficient to give each person a task for which they are responsible and pay him or her for their time?

Kerry Gleeson, in *The Personal Efficiency Program* (2004), writes on the importance in the military of discipline at an individual level for organizational success and points out that an individual soldier who fails to keep their weapon clean and functional at all times risks their own life and the lives of others if the gun jams at a moment of conflict. Likewise, intricate machinery is only as good as its weakest component. If any one individual is not working effectively, the whole organization may suffer.

The other day I had to call the technical support service of a manufacturing company. I spoke first to a general enquiries receptionist, who was polite and friendly. She put me through to another number from which I had to select from a variety of options, which then resulted in another automated response. Finally I spoke to someone who should have been able to answer my query. However, this person appeared to be having a bad day and answered the telephone as if this were my fault. Despite my efforts to be good humoured and helpful, his conduct remained unchanged throughout our conversation. Regardless of the pleasant manner of the receptionist and the clarity and efficiency of the automated dialling menus, my overall experience of contact with this well-known company was indelibly coloured by the inability of one individual to manage their actions and reactions appropriately.

Weapons *do* jam and people *do* have bad days, of course they do. And an organization that invests in the personal effectiveness of each individual will be able to expend less effort on managing these defects and more on achieving their goals.

Why Are We Ineffective in the First Place?

The second law of thermodynamics states that, in any natural cyclical process, entropy will either increase or remain the same – or, in other words, nature inclines towards disorder. So it is with our effectiveness; without constant vigilance and the application of effort, our habits either lapse or become destructive.

Habits come from positive intentions. For example, people start to smoke for a variety of reasons. Some may want to adhere to the mores of a particular social group; others may be looking for ways to manage stress responses; or to provide themselves with an alternative to snacking in an effort to lose weight. Any of these motivations in themselves are not damaging. I have never yet spoken to a smoker who claims to have smoked their first cigarette in order to risk their health. Yet the practice (and the nicotine) can quickly become a powerful and destructive addiction.

In order to maintain the focus on the original goal, regular reviews of the tactics employed and their impact are essential. There are other ways for the smoker to fit in, to combat anxiety or to lose excess pounds, which will almost certainly all be more beneficial to the smoker in the longer term. So in order to examine personal effectiveness as it can be addressed in a learning environment, this chapter will look at goals, motivation and some tools and tactics for achieving the targets.

Beginning with the End in Mind

We may be very busy, we may be very efficient, but we will also be truly effective only when we begin with the end in mind.

Stephen R. Covey (Writer and Management Consultant)

Mark was called into a meeting with some colleagues. They were planning a day conference and wanted to tap into Mark's expertise regarding the practicalities of their event. The date (around two months from the meeting) was set and had been published, the venue booked and ideas were being batted around regarding logistics. Mark listened for a few minutes to a conversation about coffee and sandwiches and then spoke up. He apologized if he had missed something, but what exactly was the conference for? The meeting became rather tense. Eventually it was decided that, while the capacity was there to make the event happen in the short amount of time available, it would be a waste of all resources because the goal had not been defined.

Mark has the drive and perseverance to be extremely busy. His time management is impressive and, for the most part, he remains calm. But what makes him particularly effective in his role is not his energy and cool-headedness; it is his ability to focus his efforts on the goal. *He begins every task with the end in mind.*

Focusing on the goal is in itself a huge topic with a wealth of scope for the creative facilitator. However, unless you've already spent some time and effort on doing this for *yourself*, you may find it difficult to elicit this kind of information from others. It's worth mentioning here, though, that you don't *have* to be a shining role model with all the answers and everything sorted in your own life in order to facilitate effective enquiries and experiences in others!

Practitioner's Enquiries

What are your own goals, both personal and professional?

Do you have goals in the short, medium and longer terms?

How effective are you in concentrating your efforts on these? What gets in the way?

Write the answers to these questions down and then consider: how easy were these questions to answer honestly?

Personal effectiveness must be about achieving goals, and so defining these goals clearly must come first.

What do You Really Want?

It is not every day that we are given the space and opportunity to consider what we, as individuals, want. Whether that be in relation to our professional role, our careers or our lives outside of the workplace, it is rare that we are asked what we want in any sense other than the superficial offerings of hospitality.

Ray Kinsella: *So what do you want?*

Terence Mann: *I want them to stop looking to me for answers, begging me to speak again, write again, be a leader. I want them to start thinking for themselves. I want my privacy.*

Ray Kinsella: *No, I mean, what do you WANT? [Gestures to the concession stand they're in front of]*

Terence Mann: *Oh. Dog and a beer.*

Field of Dreams (1989)

   Many 'activities' in the area of personal effectiveness will naturally then centre on reflection and discussion. But we sometimes forget that allowing a group of individuals the time and space to consider, disclose and discuss what they want can be a powerful experience in itself.

   Frequently, in my role as a coach or facilitator, I have begun sessions like this by asking people what their life would be like if it were perfect, or how they want their life to be. Because we are generally unaccustomed to answering questions like this, it can aid the conversation to have some kind of tangible reference point for these discussions: a range of postcards; paper and coloured pencils for them to draw; modelling clay or play dough that can be moulded; a range of objects from which to select something representative. Of course these are only starting points for reflection and conversation but the launch pad is very helpful. Another approach which works well is presenting people with binary choices: for example, would you rather your home was like coffee or peppermint tea? Would you like your job to be like a cheetah or a dolphin? The associations that people have around these choices are as varied as the people themselves and it is, of course, unimportant what they choose and why, so long as it provides a catalyst for reflection and conversation. Beware though of loading the options with value judgements and biased descriptions; asking someone whether they would rather be like an evil scuttling cockroach or a graceful, elegant swan is rarely going to be useful (although a comparison between a cockroach and a slug could provide some interesting insight).

Action to be effective must be directed to clearly conceived ends.

Jawaharlal Nehru (Indian Statesman)

Once people have their broad goals, the ability to make those goals tangible and concrete is invaluable. The model of SMART objectives (Doran, 1981) is well-known and has been adapted from the original, corporate objective-setting framework where the acronym was comprised of 'Specific', 'Measurable', 'Assignable', 'Realistic' and 'Time-related'. I have seen the 'A' signifying 'achievable', 'agreed', 'ambitious' and 'appropriate'; and I've seen the 'R' signifying 'realistic' or 'relevant'. What I believe essential to the use of the SMART objective framework in a personal effectiveness context is that the goals are specific.

As a creative trainer, any of the experiences in this book (or given in the suggested readings after the final chapter) can be utilized to get at SMART-er planning. When groups say that they need to do 'some research' on an issue, therein lies an ideal opportunity to raise the notion of precise goal-setting.

Regardless of circumstance, if an individual is to move closer towards effectiveness, then, 'What do I want?' needs to become, 'What precisely do I want to achieve and what parameters affect my ability to reach that goal?'

Practitioner's Enquiries

If you wanted to facilitate a goal-setting workshop solely for yourself, how would you do it?

What can you learn from this answer to help you design an effective goal-setting session for another individual?

How could you extrapolate your strategies here to run a workshop for a number of individuals?

How would working on an individual's life-effectiveness goals differ to an intervention for a workplace team?

People can reach a certain level of effectiveness by simply stating some precise goals and moving towards achieving them. However, in order to reach a higher level of effectiveness, people need to have a degree of self-awareness and be attuned to their own needs, reactions and responses as well as to other peoples.

Like What You're Doing Not Just Where You're Going

Life is not always the proverbial bowl of cherries. We know this and we make decisions sometimes that we will live in less than ideal circumstances sometimes in order to gain what we want in time. It may not be lovely, enjoyable or restful to live in a house undergoing alterations, but the end result will be worth temporary discomfort. However, it is one thing to tolerate the process once, but a very different matter for the builder to be uncomfortable with construction sites.

Like what you do, if you don't like it, do something else.

Paul Harvey (Broadcaster)

Enjoying what you do and finding the process satisfying can be a goal in itself. Not a 'final destination' type goal in the way, 'I will be promoted in two years' time' might be, but a desirable state of being nonetheless. If what I do on a daily basis is not satisfying or enjoyable, I will not be as effective as I could be. It may be that changing my activity, my job or even my whole career may be necessary in order to achieve optimum personal effectiveness.

It is surely preferable for an organization to be staffed by motivated, effective people, than by people motivated only by a sense of duty or the contents of their figurative or literal pay packet. If the round holes in the organization are filled with round pegs, rather than even well-meaning square ones, the function of the whole establishment will be optimized.

Different Goals for Different People

What may be a wonderful goal for some people will not help others to maximize their effectiveness at all – this is not a 'one-size-fits-all' approach. One individual may want to work towards promotion because their ambition is to be a leader in the field. Another individual has different priorities and will work more effectively when they do not carry responsibility for others.

The same is true for the methods in which effectiveness can be realized. For some people, being organized means having everything filed away in an alphabetized system. For others, it may mean having everything to hand that they need for the six projects on which they are working this week. Being personally effective in a given role is not simply about following a list of carefully unified protocols (unless the workplace task depends on doing just that), it is about working in a way that works towards a goal that is appealing.

Practitioner's Enquiries

Do you know how *you* work best? How do you know? What else have you tried?

Where and when do *you* work most effectively? How do you *know*?

How could you most effectively encourage other people to explore these issues?

How could you use individual structured enquiries such as these in a group setting?

What parallels could you utilize between a group's effectiveness and an individual's?

How could you use, for example, paired observation and feedback?

What is the benefit to an organization if people who are in the wrong role realize this and change roles or leave?

Understanding Your Own Purpose

If effectiveness then is both knowing what you want and the ecology of this goal with regard to yourself and others, these factors must be derived from something deeper. If the goals are the 'what' and the surrounding ecology and the methods by which we attain our objectives are the 'how' then both of these will be governed by the 'why' of our organizational and personal lives – in other words, our *raison d'être*.

> *It is not more vacation we need – it is more vocation.*
>
> Eleanor Roosevelt (US First Lady)

Recently I was talking to a group of trainee consultants about my business. They came up with a variety of different ways in which I could expand my client base, but I was very uncomfortable with almost everything they suggested. They had asked me all sorts of questions about my current practice and based their suggestions on perceived gaps, they hadn't suggested anything that was illegal or unethical in any way and most of the ideas were workable, so they found it hard to understand why I was less than receptive to their insight. The one question they hadn't asked was *why* I do what I do; and therefore what was my driving force. Had I followed their suggestions, I may have increased my client base, but would I have been more effective if I had left behind the vision and values that led me to embark on my current journey?

Stephen Covey, author of the best-selling *Seven Habits of Highly Effective People* (2004), once wrote that, 'Management is efficiency in climbing the ladder of success; leadership determines whether the ladder is leaning against the right wall.' Personal effectiveness, which could also be thought of as leadership of oneself, starts with identifying your own right wall and ensuring your ladder is firmly fixed against it. Of course, the same applies to organizational effectiveness – the number of organizations who invest time and money in the development of a 'corporate vision' or 'mission statement' is testament to this.

Practitioner's Enquiries

Is there a place in the workplace for discussion of personal 'drivers'?

What is the value to the organization of its members discovering and articulating their own motivations?

How could a group setting benefit the individual in helping them to explore this area?

What would *your* personal mission statement be?

How could you encourage teams or individuals to create their own effectiveness mission statement? (See the apian example in the opening section for how this process can be more powerful and meaningful.)

Understanding Our Place in a Wider Ecology

As we explored in Chapter 3, it is rare that any of us work, or live, truly in isolation. Our actions and reactions have an impact on others and being aware of that impact and managing our actions accordingly is a significant part of being effective as an individual in a social world.

When we live or work closely with other people, we are provided with hundreds of examples of the impact we have on others. Noticing the way that people relate to us and the relationship between our actions and their reactions can give the effective individual plenty of data from which to draw conclusions about their impact. Given the opportunity and the inclination we can choose to reflect upon these and alter our future behaviours accordingly.

If we decide to change our behaviour, we can either do so based on an assumptive inference ('Lisa is annoyed, I must have upset her') or we can base our actions on a conversation with the other person. ('Lisa, is there something I've done that has upset you?')

> People are beginning to realise that success takes more than intellectual excellence or technical prowess, and that we need another sort of skill just to survive – and certainly to thrive – in the increasingly turbulent job market of the future. Internal qualities such as resilience, initiative, optimism and adaptability are taking on new valuation.
>
> Daniel Goleman (Academic and Writer)

Goleman (1996 and 1999 after Salovey and Mayer, 1990) describes a number of skills and qualities which increase a person's effectiveness both in and outside of the workplace: self-awareness; self-management; motivation; empathy; and managing relationships.

Competence in these areas allows individuals to be fully cognisant of themselves and of others around them. While it is difficult to 'teach' these skills, it is relevant to introduce the concepts and to provide activities which are designed to give participants the opportunities to practise and explore them. As always, start with your own experience and feelings first.

Interpersonal Effectiveness Opportunities for the Creative Trainer

The question here is how can the development of interpersonal effectiveness be facilitated within an artificial experiential learning environment? Is it reasonable to expect that an authentic understanding of one's own real ecology could be elicited from an unreal environment? We believe that, while there is clearly no real substitute for ongoing reflection and feedback, it is possible to draw valuable insight from the training-room environment.

Any activity designed for groups can be used to look at interpersonal effectiveness. Activities increase in validity as learning experiences when people feel real emotions: genuine excitement; irritation; anxiety; exasperation; (dis)satifaction. People are more likely to respond authentically in an unreal environment when placed under increased pressure, so you as a facilitator can adapt any task to achieve this result in a variety

---

Practitioners' Enquiries

How aware are you of how you feel and what has elicited those feelings?

When tensions rise, how able are you to act rationally, rather than being at the mercy of your immediate responses?

What drives you? Can you capture this to increase your motivation for daily tasks?

Do you understand easily why other people respond as they do?

When you look at your working relationships, are you successful in relating to others in a productive and effective way?

How do you measure/understand the impact you have on others?

How much do you assume? How much is real?

How could you use the way in which such data is measured and collected in an artificial experiential environment?

---

of ways. Pressure can be increased by decreasing the time allowed for an activity, by increasing the quality required, or the quantity of concrete outputs. The stakes of an activity can be raised by introducing a need to 'pass' in some way, with consequences for failure to do so.

People tend to feel differently about activities if the targets change: it could be that what had been an enjoyable pastime becomes stressful if an element of competition is added, or in fact if that competitive edge is removed. I once ran a very simple activity for a group of people who worked together on a daily basis and knew one another well. There were two phases of the task, and I asked them to complete the first phase of preparation and planning in two sub-groups. Several participants made the assumption that the task was going to be a competition. When, at the end of the first phase, I asked the two groups to join together in implementation, the whole activity fell apart due to the disappointment in the more competitive members that they were not going to have the opportunity to 'win'. This anti-climax was so intense for them that pursuing the activity was futile. Nonetheless, the discrepancy between the views of the group as a whole contributed to a powerful learning conversation afterwards.

There are clearly ethical issues with pressurizing people in any form and we have written about this more generally in the opening section of the book. However, this debate is particularly pertinent when you as a facilitator are in a position to *emotionally* manipulate those involved. I find the foremost principle to bear in mind is simply this:

What level of emotion is necessary for the learning to take place?

Capturing Interpersonal Effectiveness Lessons

If they are to be productive, reviews of interpersonal effectiveness-related exercises should always focus on precisely what happened and what individuals could do differently in similar circumstances. You could use questions such as these:

- How did you feel when X happened?
- After X minutes, there were voices raised. What was going on then?
- What could you [individual participant's name] do differently in a difficult situation?
- What would you need to help you do that?
- How effective did you allow each other to be? What could have increased your effectiveness?

It's worth revisiting the opening section of the book about how to review an exercise to help prepare yourself to extract the maximum amount of insight from such discussions.

One of the great aspects of focusing on individual behaviours is that, for the most part, everyone has experienced the full spectrum of reactions. Therefore, a really useful way of tapping in to this experience in an artificial learning environment is to use a 'fishbowl' technique (see David Jaques' book *Learning in Groups* (1984) for a range of ideas and strategies like this to help people learn together). Fishbowling constitutes an inner ring of participants undertaking a task whilst surrounded by an outer ring of observers. These are able to focus on the process that is unfolding instead of being caught up in the activity. This method has the advantage that an individual can experience their own effectiveness (or otherwise) in a given situation and the observers have a completely different, but equally illuminating, objective experience.

Interpersonal Effectiveness Exercise Idea – Paired Effectiveness

This process takes about an hour (plus overall review) and requires two short exercises. Both should be about 15 minutes in length. One should be a physical-style task and the other a conversational or discursive task.*

Physical task ideas: Building the highest possible tower of straws and lollipop sticks; building a glider from paper plates and tissue paper; creating a prototype for a gadget to make their work easier. In essence anything that requires them to *do* something.

Discursive task ideas: Have the group nominate and agree on which celebrities should make up the next governmental cabinet; ask the group to debate the pros and cons of a controversial issue (GM crops, animal testing for medical purposes, religious education in state schools, abolishing the monarchy); the classic prioritizing of items to be salvaged from a plane crash in the desert and so on. In essence anything that requires them to *talk about* something.

The exercise set-up: Start by asking the group as a whole to define 'effectiveness'. Press for as much detail as possible: What is the difference between effectiveness and efficiency? What does it mean to be effective in a group? and so on.

Split the group into two halves: half participants and half observers. Equal numbers are useful but not essential. Ensure that everyone gets observed at some point, even if it means that the trainer takes an observer role. Place participants in the centre of the room and have the observers around the edge of the room so that they a clear sight line to the participant opposite them. Ensure each observer is observing a different participant.

Brief the observers that they are going to observe a group undertake a task. Instruct them that they must notice and note down specifically:

a) what the group is doing that makes them particularly effective as a unit;

b) what their particular participant is doing with regard to the factors of effectiveness that you drew up before the commencement of the exercise.

It may be worth briefing them to focus on what people are doing, what they are saying and how they are saying it if the group have little experience in observing other people. They will probably need to write notes for themselves.

Part One

Next introduce the participants to the practical task. Get them underway and then step back.

Halfway through the allotted 15 minutes stop the exercise. Then bring together the observer and participant. Ask them to talk for five minutes as a pair about what the observer has noticed of the group as a whole, and specifically of their partner. Ask them to discuss what the task-participant could do immediately to increase their effectiveness in relation to the task.

Then bring the participants back to the centre of the room and restart the task. The task then continues till the end of the allotted time.

Recombine the observer and participant for a short (maximum two minute) discussion about the changes implemented following their first conversation.

Part Two

Ask the observers to sit in the centre and participants to sit at the edge of the room. They now change roles. Brief the new observers as above.

Introduce the discursive task to the new participants. Repeat the process exactly as outlined in Part One, pausing the discussion part way through for five minutes of paired observer feedback.

The Review

Bring the sub-groups together and ask them to discuss these type of questions:

Is personal effectiveness in task different from interpersonal effectiveness in process?

What were the different sorts of effectiveness required in the tasks?

How effective were any given individuals in relation to any other?

How easy was it to change your effectiveness quickly (in light of any feedback)?

How did individual's effectiveness differ before and after feedback?

Did the feedback help? (Given that if I intensively focus on one element of my behaviour consciously, I may neglect other areas.)

How did each individual's effectiveness change impact on the group dynamic as a whole?

How did it feel to be an observer of process? What's the useful transferable learning here?

Note: * We first used this process idea on a programme that was jointly developed with Drs J. McDonald and D. Filipović-Carter, and their contribution here is acknowledged.

Why Do People Behave Differently, Really?

When exploring interpersonal effectiveness, trainers tend to seek out observable behaviours of the kind that are provided by Goleman (1996 and 1999). However, while this may give us the 'what', it does not provide the 'why' behind behaviour and therefore can frequently leave learners dissatisfied, as specific observations are highly context dependent. Giving an individual feedback such as, 'You'd be more effective if you took a greater active part in the debate' is perfectly reasonable; however, if the person receiving that feedback responds with, 'I just didn't have anything to say at that point,' there is very little progress that can be made.

Personal effectiveness or ineffectiveness bleeds from one area of life to another uncontrollably. If I am focused and goal-oriented at work, I am likely to be so at home. If my life outside the workplace is littered with dysfunctional relationships, the probability

Practitioner's Enquiries

Where are you most effective and what can you take from this area of your life into another area?

Where are your learners most effective?

Do they understand what can they take from that area of life into another?

of my being able to be function well amongst my colleagues diminishes. This presents a challenge for the facilitator, as our remit is usually to focus on the workplace. However, it can be useful to ask participants to reflect on their behaviour and effectiveness both inside and outside their working environment.

Regardless of situation, we tend to act according to the same general principles and approaches. We don't always do things the same way, but we have a general preference that *influences* but does not *dictate* our behaviour (Briggs-Meyers and Meyers, 1980).

Practitioner's Enquiries

In the semi-controlled atmosphere of the workplace, what are the ways in which you notice people's behaviours differing most?

Which kinds of activities reveal those differences most acutely?

How can you recreate those settings in a training room?

How could you help people to address those differences in a constructive and non-judgemental manner?*

How might you best help learners to capture their insights so that they can use them in the future?

Note: * One resource we both find useful here is *The Feedback Game©*, developed by Peter Gerrickens (1998).

Differing Behaviours – Exercise Idea

Use the Top Quality Toy Company Exercise from Chapter 8. This exercise provides sufficient scope for individuals within groups to demonstrate an array of behavioural preferences.

Then review using the areas of difference below.

How do people relate to the people around them? Are they thinking things through by talking and discussion? Are they diving in to an activity and planning as they are touching the physical components? Or are they later to come into discussion then contributing more fully formed ideas? Is their approach to the activity more reflective?

What kind of information are they paying most attention to? Are they detail-oriented, relying on current and past experience to form their perspective? Are they focusing more on the big picture, relying on inspiration, and reading between the lines to provide their view of the activity?

What criteria are they using to make decisions? Logic and objective criteria, or are people and compassion consistently more important? What kind of language are they using? Are they talking about what they 'think' or are they more likely to discuss how they 'feel'?

How are they organizing themselves? Do they have a scheduled, planning-focused approach, eyes always on the impending deadline, and possibly anxious if time is short. Or are they thriving under the pressure of deadlines, resistant to deciding on a strategy too early and still producing ideas up until the last minute?

The value of this kind of conversation is in the realizations that people who respond differently in the same situation are not necessarily 'wrong' but simply approaching the task from an alternative position. For example, if I become aware that I am likely to look always to the details, I will value more highly the contribution of my colleagues who are drawn to the bigger picture, rather than seeing their observations as impractical. Thus we are potentially able to work together with less tension and in doing so increasing both of our effectiveness.

Self-awareness, and awareness of others (and flexibility) however, only goes so far and certainly does not inexorably lead to effectiveness. In order for self-awareness to aid effectiveness, it must be a foundation for goal-oriented action.

The Five Cs

Give a girl the right shoes and she can conquer the world.

Marilyn Monroe (Actress)

A former colleague of mine bases all she does on sound principles, on preparation, evidence and consultation with experts where appropriate. And if she needs to do something about which she is anxious, on top of all other preparation, she wears 'The Red Shoes'. Contrary to office lore, 'the red shoes' do not have magic powers. They do not change anything, apart from how she feels as she walks into a room.

We all find ways in which to cope with situations we find challenging. It may be a physical device like red shoes. Or it may be that we have rituals or habits which make us able to function more effectively.

We believe personal effectiveness comes in five main areas, all illustrated opposite. Alongside a brief description is a selection of questions that a facilitator can ask learners in order to help reflection on each area.

The fact that people are all solely responsible for their own effectiveness is a gift to the facilitator of artificial experiential learning. It means that any activity at all can be given a twist to enable people to experiment with adapting their own behaviour in an environment that is safe and free from real-life consequences.

To what extent an individual can consciously manage their reactions in a given situation offers some interesting territory for the creative trainer. This kind of work is often done through the use of 'role-play' – frequently to the chagrin of the participants, whose skin often begins to crawl the moment the concept of role-play is discussed. While playing a role can offer useful learning opportunities, the unconstructive reaction can negate the advantage. Therefore, rather than suggesting activities which rely on a fake present, the ideas opposite utilize the participants' authentic past experience.

	Facilitator Questions
Confidence	
In order to be truly effective, we need to believe we can achieve our goal, in every area of our lives. Positive and constructive feedback, personal coaching and the achievement of realistic goals can all help an individual to increase their confidence and therefore be more resourceful and effective.	What have you achieved recently? Following a participant's decision to take a specified action: Will you do this, really? What is it that makes you sure/unsure of this? What will you need to achieve this? How will it feel to have it done? What could get in the way?
Change	
We need to be able to adapt quickly when our circumstances change if we are going to be effective regardless of context; being aware of where we have the control or influence to take fruitful, effective action and where acceptance and rest are better options is a short cut to having more energy to focus towards our goals.	When was the last time you found yourself feeling frustrated? What did you do? Think of your workplace. What is within your control to alter? What could you improve? Who has authority to instigate change in your workplace? How could you influence their decisions?
Communications	
As we interact with people who have different preferences, agendas and backgrounds. In order to work effectively with others we must learn to communicate fully with a wide range of other people.	Think about the people that you interact with regularly. What works in terms of communication for some and not for others? How do you like people to ask you to do something? How do you like them to show appreciation for a task well done?
Constant Learning	
Effectiveness is not something that can be achieved and then will always remain. If we are not constantly looking for opportunities to learn, able to review the outcomes and the impact of our actions and reactions and make choices regarding how to behave in similar circumstances in the future, we will not maintain an effective approach.	How can you ensure you learn from new experiences? Which experiences do you tend to learn from most? What is the learning in X experience for you/ your group?
Coping	
Day-to-day effectiveness often relies on using tactics such as discerning what is essential activity and what is peripheral and acting accordingly;* and the ability to make good 'coalface' decisions which align with wider goals, in order that every action and reaction is effective.	How do you prioritize your activity at work? How could you organize your diary more effectively? What resources are available to you in your workplace that would increase your effectiveness? What would you need to do to make use of these?

Note: * An excellent resource here is Stephen Covey's *Time Management Matrix* (Covey, 2004:151ff).

Three Personal Effectiveness Reflection Activity Ideas

---

1. Hindsight Remote Control

Split the group into pairs. Taking turns, each partner describes a real conflict situation in their workplace.

Then partner A goes through their conflict situation a second time, this time partner B should pause the description three times in order to discuss how partner A could have behaved differently to achieve a different result – as if with the remote control of hindsight. For example, 'How could you have expressed yourself differently then?' 'What might have been the result?'

Note: It must *always* be partner A's behaviour under discussion, *not* the other party's.

Then the process is repeated with partner B's conflict.

Review around what is within our control and influence, even when the conflict is apparently someone else's 'fault'. How can we be effective in other people's ineffectiveness?

If 'hindsight remote control' focuses on an individual's effectiveness when in conflict with other people, the following exercise is more about effectiveness in isolation – in a situation when we have total control as it is all about our own behaviour.

---

2. I *Always* Do That...

As individuals, encourage people to remember a situation when they have done something and afterwards figuratively kicked themselves and said (words to the effect of) 'Arrgh, I always do that!'

Put people into pairs. partner A describes the situation in detail to partner B, who acts according to A's direction. B must ask for complete detail in order to experience A's memory, and A must mine their memory for every detail, thus providing both with full information through the modelling of the ineffective behaviour.

Then the pair uses all that information to discern the landscape around an ineffective behaviour, the recurring mistake. In what particular situations is it likely to occur? What are the signs it's coming? At what point could a different tack be chosen and a different behaviour displayed? What might that different behaviour look like? What might result?

Then swap and repeat for partner B's experience.

Review around what the learning is here. What insight does it give partner B to have partner A living their mistake/experience and vice versa? What could be changed? Do you have the will to change this habitual reaction or behaviour? And so on.

The two exercises above focus on an intense reliving of an actual experience. The activity below requires participants to look at their experience and values more generally by learning from the experience and example of a person they admire.

---

3. Historical Figure

A week before the intervention, ask participants to find and bring with them a picture of the historical figure they most admire. This should preferably be someone most people have heard of, although what is significant here is that the participant who has chosen them should admire the figure because they know *about* them, rather than having *known* them. This way the historical figure can be held as an inspirational icon rather than a human being with failings and phases of ineffectiveness.

Then, in small groups, discuss situations in which participants would particularly like to be more effective. After a brief description of the situation, their chosen historical figure and their reasons for selecting them, the key question to ask is, 'What would [admired historical figure] do in this situation?' 'What could you learn from this?'

The beauty of this exercise is that then the participants may take their pictures away again, to be used as a tangible reminder and inspiration for other situations.

As mentioned in the opening paragraph of this chapter, personal effectiveness is not the easiest area for which to create artificial learning experiences. Whether conversation and reflection constitutes an experience in itself or not remains a moot point; and we do not seek to provide the answer to that here. However, what is true is that any experience can be targeted to encouraging the learners to reflect upon, explore and build on their own effectiveness. The following chapter examines how experiential learning can provide opportunities to do this in a changing environment.

6 *Dealing with Change*

It may be hard for an egg to turn into a bird: it would be a jolly sight harder for it to learn to fly while remaining an egg. We are like eggs at present. And you cannot go on indefinitely being just an ordinary, decent egg. We must be hatched or go bad.

C.S. Lewis (Writer)

Our individual and organizational ability to adapt to changed circumstances has a huge effect on our performance. As facilitators, our role in this process is varied. The exercises given in Chapter 4 on leadership provide ample opportunities to explore how a leader can most effectively instigate and manage change.[1] This chapter is not concerned with the *why* of change. Instead it will look at ways to allow for the development of skills in the dealing with change as it happens.

Changing Philosophy

I worked in my last job role for five years. During that time I had four line managers. At different times I worked directly with one, two, three and four colleagues. At one point there was only one person in the hierarchy between me and the head of department, at another there were three. I worked in four different offices; in one I was alone and in another I shared with ten others.

Change is a fact in the majority of professional lives. It cannot be otherwise and, to a large extent, most people accept and deal with this certainty without it causing them too many problems. We may not like it, especially when we are enjoying life the way it is, but we accept it as we accept the change in seasons and quickly become accustomed to our new conditions. Sometimes changes are due to circumstances outside of the work content – a manager goes on maternity leave and their responsibilities are shared amongst others as appropriate; or someone leaves and is replaced. But there are many times when changes in the workplace are a result of a conscious decision by one or more persons in authority and are intended to help the organization, in C.S. Lewis's words, to fly.

Here's a confession: I am not by nature keen on change. I just like things to work and when they are functioning I have a tendency towards an 'if it ain't broke, don't fix it' approach. However, if I am aware that, by doing something differently, a better outcome can be achieved, then I will put my whole self behind the implementation of that change. This can make me sensitive to the needs of those who are unwilling to wholeheartedly and unquestioningly embrace change, but I am aware that sometimes

---

1   See *Inspiring Leadership* by John Adair (2002) for a great exploration of the place of leaders in change.

my own tendency towards cynicism will temper the way I work with others. Sometimes as facilitators managing ourselves out of the equation can be an important step.

Practitioner's Enquiries

What do you need, yourself, in order to embrace change?

Are you the kind of person who is likely implement change 'just to shake things up a little'?

If so, what are the pros and cons of such behaviour?

If not, how do you respond to people who do this? If you are, how do you feel towards those who have a more cautious approach?

As a facilitator, how does your own response to change impact how you might plan and run an intervention?

Change in Organizations

When an organization[2] undergoes change, the decision to implement a modification or even a revolution is always made by some people and imposed upon others – with a greater or lesser degree of consultation. The same is true for the form that change will take and how it will be implemented. How people react to change imposed upon them will depend on a number of different factors which will include (but not be limited to) their loyalty to the organization/leader as well as their security regarding their position and expertise, their personality and their understanding of the goal. What is common to almost everyone, however, is that news of an impending change will bring with it some level of anxiety.

> *The organisational-change bandwagon seems to have gotten out of control. And those who are riding it are scared.*
> Bob Filipczak (Journalist) quoted in *The Challenge of Change in Organizations*

Of course, not every change is big or particularly frightening. Whilst we thrive in stable conditions, human beings are resilient creatures and are able to adapt well to changes such as driving a different car or sporting a new hairstyle. These straightforward changes may cause us momentary discomfort ('Oops, that's not the indicator, that's the windscreen wipers!') but we are familiar with changes of this magnitude and are confident that a little practice will render the new as established and so anxiety is minimal. In the workplace, this kind of change could be something like using new software. It doesn't represent a policy alteration of any kind, simply an essentially cosmetic change. Such small changes, and the feelings associated with them, offer the creative trainer a wealth of possible material.

---

2   There's a large body of literature about the theory of change. If you're interested in getting an overview of the area, a great place to start is The Impact Factory website and specifically the section entitled Managing Change in Others: www.impactfactory.com.

Dealing With Change Exercise Idea – 'Card Sort'

Split your group into two and give each a shuffled deck of cards.

Then give the simple brief that each of the two teams are to 'sort the cards': they have one minute to plan how they are going to do this, but the actual sorting must be conducted in silence. The aim is to do this as fast as possible – in some settings it is appropriate to offer a small prize to the winner.

Record the time that each team takes to complete the task and then hold a discussion around planning, implementation and quality – after all, 'sort the cards' as an instruction is at best nebulous. It could be argued that simply squaring the deck of cards would suffice.

Give the groups one minute to re-plan, for increased efficiency and then inform them that the time to silently sort starts now. After a few seconds of silent sorting, step in and change the rules with any instruction. For example: Aces are now universally low; the picture cards are now to be ordered (low to high) Queen – King – Jack; all diamond cards must be set at right angles to the rest of the pack. *Have these changes ready prepared on a flipchart for an instant reveal.* The group must react to this change in silence.

Review around people's reactions to the change, how flexible their plans were, how it felt to be deprived of the ability to appeal, and so on.

It could be, as in the exercise given above, that a change requires the team to tackle a familiar task in a new way. For example, change in the workplace might involve altering the way in which employees are asked to prepare for meetings. Instead of simply attending a meeting and presenting an oral report, it may be required that reports are written and provided to the meeting's chairperson several days in advance of the meeting. The content of the report could be the same, as is the requirement that each attendee provides information. While everyone may be convinced that this will provide quicker and more effective meetings, the change may still meet with a little resistance because it requires an *old habit* to be put to one side in order that a new practice may emerge.

Practitioner's Enquiries

If you're asked to provide an intervention to help people deal with change, what kinds of changes does the client have in mind?

What level of anxiety or resistance are you likely to be dealing with?

Has the change already happened, is it currently being implemented, is it planned? Or is this intervention desired to help people deal with change more generally?

There are occasions when it is accepted that some kind of behavioural change needs to take place in order to achieve a desired outcome, and yet those impacted by the change are uncertain what exactly this behavioural change should or even could be. Everyone may agree that the whole team's performance would improve if only they could stop criticizing each other's contributions, but this operational utopia seems unattainable without an unrealistic (not to mention undesirable) policed censorship.

Changing Beliefs

It is not the strongest of the species that survive, nor the most intelligent, but the one most responsive to change.

Attributed to both Charles Darwin (Naturalist)
and Clarence Darrow (Lawyer and Civil Libertarian)

Beliefs have a startlingly conservative effect on behaviour: there are times when I believe so strongly that I *know*, without a shadow of doubt, that I cannot do something. I *know* I cannot run a marathon, so I will not do it, nor even try to do it. It may be true that if I attempted to run a marathon today the attempt would end badly; but if I challenge the belief that I cannot do it by incrementally building up both confidence and fitness, who knows what may be possible? When we *know* something can never happen, it is necessary to look at why we *believe* that to be the case. This is where change can be extremely challenging. Not only our behaviour but our beliefs – the threads from which our perception of reality is woven – need to be confronted and possibly amended if change is to take place. Again, having groups challenge established beliefs and assumptions, however small these may be, offers considerable opportunity when planning a creative intervention. After all, if *one* belief can be challenged and debunked, what is stopping *any* belief from being similarly challenged? If one can look at beliefs for what they are rather than blindly accepting them as immutable facts, one can take control over them. We can choose to maintain our beliefs or we can challenge them.

Sometimes a change is one I have no control over, or one that is imposed upon me. The imposition could be made by a superior, by a colleague or friend, or by – for want of a better phrase – the universe. A superior can decree that from a given date, all hours worked must be entered on a timesheet; or that I must move my desk from one office to another. My only choice in this situation is to continue working in the changed conditions, or to tender my resignation. A colleague could leave my workplace for another, a friend could relocate to another city, and I have control over neither situation but the impact of the change upon me is still acute. An earthquake, volcano or flood could rob me of my home; I could be bereaved; an accident or illness could render me unable to continue my lifestyle. We can embrace change, tolerate it, resist it or just accept it, but the fact is that we must learn to deal with it in positive ways if we are to thrive within changeable organizations.

Barger and Kirby (1995) in *The Challenge of Change in Organizations*, use the metaphor of a pioneering journey to illustrate what occurs when people face change. Their metaphorical journey has a number of stages in change transition: the decision to leave; the leaving of the old way; preparation for the new; the transition itself; and the establishment of new behaviours.

Practitioner's Exercise

What specific factors allow a person to deal well with imposed change?

Write ten skills/qualities which combine to allow a person to function productively in a changing environment.

How might a training intervention access these types of skills and qualities most effectively?

Might these factors differ depending on the source of the imposition of change? How might you need to deal with these factors differently? What principles would remain the same?

Are you requiring that change comes from within a group in order to function effectively, or are you imposing change upon them? Both internal and external drivers offer possibilities, and both can be very powerful forces in a learning environment.

This metaphor can be helpful, especially as there is no real sense in Barger and Kirby's work of arriving at a place where change is a thing of the past. Arrival is only the notion that this *particular* journey is at an end. In all organizations, change is a constant process and any final destination is never reached.

When you're finished changing, you're finished.

Benjamin Franklin (US President)

As a training practitioner, it is useful to know *where* on a change journey the group is, in order to make the intervention most pertinent. If they are in the early stages of the change process, it is necessary to fully describe the later, more difficult, stages. We have both run many courses for people setting out on research projects and know (both from our own experience and from the experience of working with hundreds of people who have followed the same path) that such programmes are fraught with potential hazards. A major and ubiquitous hazard in this case occurs in the middle phase where novelty of the project has worn off, the end is not yet in sight and many people have difficult periods of wondering either if they are able to carry on or indeed if they want to. But when working with people who are enthusiastically embarking on their project, how wise is it, indeed how useful is it, to potentially discourage them with tales of hardships to come? Does the risk of discouragement balance the return of letting someone know what lies in store, and that it is not a problem unique to them?

An experiential parallel here is the often-used 'cross the river using planks and boxes without touching the water' (with the various caveats imposed by the trainer) task. Any team can get *most* way through the exercise with little trouble, but the *real* obstacle is the lack of planning at the start and the fact that some kit has been spent (and so the task has changed) midway through the exercise.

Here is our version of this change exercise which requires less kit, space and time.

Change Exercise – Group Solitaire

Use the traditional game of marble solitaire (see Figure 6.1). The aim of the game is to end up with a single marble (or counter) in the centre of the board, the exact opposite of the starting position shown below. The marbles are eliminated by jumping over others and removing the jumped marbles.

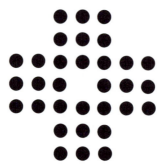

Figure 6.1   Illustration of equipment layout for 'Group Solitaire' exercise

In our version of the game, each move must be taken by consecutive team members. Give the group five minutes to develop a strategy for completing the game.

After the end of the five minute strategizing period, there must be no talking except for one-minute discussion every four minutes.*

Move the board to the far end of the room. Each participant must then approach the board alone, take their move and return to the group. Allow ten minutes for the group to make as many moves as they can.

When the full time has elapsed, review the experience with the group. Lead the review around the following topics:

Strategy versus practice

Reactions under stress

Personal aptitude versus team effort (how do people react when someone else makes an error?)

What is the learning from this activity about change?

Note: *Adapt these timings depending on the level of the group you are working with.

The bottom line here is that change is easy to simulate in a learning environment. Change the conditions, change the rules, change their roles, change the information, change the team; in fact, change anything. It's all change. Helping a group to unpack and be able to transfer to other settings what they learn from how they collectively and individually reacted to these changes is where the facilitator can become invaluable.

Whenever I am asked to facilitate a session around change, it is necessary to quickly establish how *certain* that change is. Is the change a fait accompli (and my role is merely to help smooth the transition)? Is it a possible change (and my role is to help the client to identify thoughts, feeling, reactions and possible stumbling blocks from the team)? Or is it a problem-solving type session where the team has realized that all is not right and wants to change in order to rectify the issues? In any of these situations, it is not my role to set the goals that will instigate change. Rather, once a change of some kind is proposed or announced, it is my role to enable people to manage the transition effectively.

So, regardless of the type of activities you choose to help you, as a facilitator there are three broad areas upon which you may choose to focus, namely:

- an individual's (but could also be a team's) reaction to change per se;
- the reaction to imposed change (that is, when change is driven by an external force);
- the reaction to change driven by internal factors (that is, an individual or team implements a personal change to help them achieve a goal, without any external pressures).

We shrink from change; yet is there anything that can come into being without it?

Marcus Aurelius (Roman Emperor)

With reference to Barger and Kirby's travel metaphor, regardless who has made the decision to embark on the journey, those who will be making the change need to embrace the choice to go as well as preparing to leave the security of what is familiar. Some people are, of course, more willing than others to do this.

Reactions to Change

As suggested above, creating activities enabling people to learn about and develop their reactions to change is straightforward. You can use any exercise, game or activity and simply change the rules halfway through, add a rule or a restriction, substitute or remove team members; and then review around the reactions that people have to the changing circumstances. This kind of activity does, however, lay the facilitator open to criticism; so steel yourself against irate team members who blame you for their frustrations or lack of success.

One of the frequent reactions to a changing situation is the cry of the victim, 'I've got no choice.' It is extremely rare that a workplace scenario would genuinely provide an individual with no choice: there is always, of course, the option to leave.

The great thing is, if one can, to stop regarding all the unpleasant things as interruptions in one's 'own' or 'real' life. The truth is, of course, that what one regards as interruptions are precisely one's life.

C.S. Lewis (Writer)

For those who don't take that option and remain in a changing environment within which they are not naturally comfortable, there are two options: to be as effective as possible in the situation; or to lament the changes. Lamentation looks back while effectiveness, as we have seen in Chapter 5, looks ahead to the goal.

So what is it that makes the difference between these people? We believe that there are three qualities which, if these can be developed in those undergoing change, will increase the effectiveness of those individuals and consequently of their organization:[3]

- *Resilience*: the ability to bounce back, not to focus on what has changed or failed but on what is now, and to get on with the task in hand.
- *Responsibility*: the ability to reflect on what is within one's own control and to focus one's actions here, rather than investing energy in futile activity.
- *Resourcefulness*: the awareness of all the resources that are at one's disposal; and the utilization of these.

As a training practitioner, working in artificial situations, this presents a challenge. Training sessions are essentially fairly comfortable for most people – the session runs only for a limited time, so only so much change can be possible. However, with just a few alterations to your activities, you as a facilitator are able to bring these three qualities into focus for the participants in your interventions.

Comfort, Stretch and Panic

In his work with Project Adventure, Karl Rohnke[4] based his leadership and personal development work on the notion that people learn more when they stretch themselves and their abilities. The idea of a 'comfort zone' or being 'out of one's comfort zone' has long been in common parlance, and Rohnke's model of working out of the comfort zone in order to develop has been adopted by much of the training and development fraternity. What is relevant here is that change will, almost by definition, take people out of their comfort zone. Providing there is not so much change that they begin to panic, and providing of course that the experience is reflected upon, change will almost certainly result in learning.

Practitioner's Enquiries

What can you do to place people outside of their comfort zone sufficiently to test their resilience?

How could you explore personal responsibility in a training environment?

How resourceful do your activities allow people to be? Is there sufficient scope in the instructions for people to bring imaginative or unconventional approaches to the tasks?

Do your review discussions explore the applications of these qualities? How could this be achieved most effectively?

---

3   The contribution of Drs J. McDonald and D. Filipović-Carter is acknowledged here.

4   See http://www.karlrohnke.com and http://www.wilderdom.com/projectadventure/ProjectAdventureBrief.htm for more information.

Changing Competence

Thus far, this chapter has largely dealt with externally visible changes, those perhaps imposed on a whole team or organization. However, when people need to develop their competence in a given area, they will need to experience change in themselves. Psychologist Abraham Maslow[5] is credited with developing a theory of four stages which people go through as they learn a new skill.

1. *Unconscious Incompetence*: the state before the learning of a new skill is embarked upon. (That is, 'I have no idea what this skill involves, therefore am unaware of my incompetence in it.')
2. *Conscious Incompetence*: the state when learning has commenced, but the skill is yet to be mastered. (That is, 'I have discovered how much there is to learn, and with that discovery comes the realization of the magnitude of my incompetence.')
3. *Conscious Competence*: the state when the skill has been acquired, but confidence in using it is still lacking. (That is, 'I have developed the new ability, however, while using it I am unable to focus on anything else as I remain fully conscious of my actions.')
4. *Unconscious Competence*: the state when the skill is fully mastered and confidence in using it is high. (That is, 'I have become so familiar with using my new-found skill that I am able to think of other things at the same time.')

The second and third of these stages are often uncomfortable – no one likes to feel incompetent, especially in a role in which they feel they should be well-equipped to do the task at hand. Therefore preserving resilience, responsibility and resourcefulness in this period of discomfort is the key to maintaining effectiveness.

Imposed Change – Change That Comes from Without

> *Because things are the way they are, things will not stay the way they are.*
>
> Bertolt Brecht (Poet and Playwright)

Regardless of the type of change, if the change is to be healthy it must have been predicated by a clear vision of success. Vision (as captured and relayed by a leader) was examined earlier in this book and the possession of vision is widely reported to be a key (and somewhat elite) attribute of successful and transformational leaders everywhere. *This means that most people have a professional vision or goal provided for them.* In this situation, in order to truly deal with change, one must both acknowledge what is good about what is new and what can be shed from what is old in order to make space. Transitions will be smoother and performance more likely to be maintained if all those who will be impacted upon by that change are able to embrace the goal of the change.

---

5   We've been unable to ascertain the origins of the model definitively. To appreciate our dilemma, type 'conscious competence' into a search engine.

When People Agree with the Change

Of course, when we have a change imposed upon us, the imposition does not necessarily mean that we will be resistant to the change. If we have been consulted and our views taken into account and our needs met in the change, or, better yet, if we are presented with a change which immediately appeals to us and seems like a good idea, we can be welcoming of the enforced adjustments. This happy state of affairs does not automatically mean we will find the alteration to our circumstances easy, but it does mean that our motivation will help us to find the resilience, resourcefulness and responsibility we need to remain effective.

Practitioner's Enquiries

Think of a change that came from without and that you agreed with. Why did you think it was a good idea?

Did the means by which the change was communicated to you affect the way that you responded? Why/why not?

What aspects of the change appealed to you? Did you agree with the *task* itself or the *vision*?

How could you simulate this kind of attractive change in a learning environment?

When People Don't Agree with the Change

Usually the times that we remember having a change imposed upon us are when we are not happy with the perceived or real *impact* of that change. A whole range of reactions can be present in a situation like this, and if we are not very careful we can end up sulking – not the most effective frame of mind from within which to work.

Practitioner's Enquiries

Think of a change that came from without and that you did not agree with. Why specifically did you disagree?

How was the change communicated? Did the form or style of communication make a difference?

What factors influenced your thinking specifically? Did you disagree with the *task* itself or the underpinning vision?

How did you handle the situation? What does hindsight tell you about your strategy?

How could you simulate this kind of experience in a learning environment?

Gaining learning from experiences that draw out these kinds of reactions can be challenging for some participants. The immediate response is often to either play the role of a victim, or to cast you as facilitator in the role of villain; this response in itself allows the individual to abdicate responsibility for their own actions and certainly for their own learning. What they think of you is unimportant (really!) but their learning is your primary objective, so it is always worth challenging both the 'victim' and 'villain'-type responses.

Change Exercise – Aligning with an Imposed Change

Ask the group to consider business as usual. Have them brainstorm all *disadvantages* of the existing way of doing things. Provide slips of paper, and ask that one disadvantage be written on each slip of paper. Get each group member to choose one that they will be particularly pleased to see the back of; then ask them to tear it into shreds (or burn it, if possible). Repeats are allowed, that is, more than one group member may destroy any one disadvantage.

Then have them brainstorm all the possible *advantages* of the new way. Don't allow 'yes, but' statements at all. Split the group into threes or fours, provide paper and a plethora of coloured pens and get them to design marketing posters for the new way.

Review this around how it feels to give up the disadvantageous aspects, what does this allow them to do differently/more effectively?

Then explore what is necessary in order to market the new way; how do they feel having done it? Did some people find this easier than others? In what way?

The entrepreneur always searches for change, responds to it, and exploits it as an opportunity.
Peter F. Drucker (Writer and Consultant)

The final kind of change is the one driven from an internal motivation to improve, to progress, expand or develop. When we as individuals wish to change something as a result of such an internal driver or ambition, this is rarely a cause for distress even if the changes are difficult – the motivation towards the desirable end result is sufficient. To this end, enhancing your learners' entrepreneurial talents and facilitating the development of critical and creative thinkers is the topic of the next chapter.

7 *Producing Creative and Critical Thinkers*

Malcolm: *She's a box-ticker, Hugh, she can't think outside of the box.*
Hugh: *No, in fact, she's built a box inside the actual box and she's doing*
            her thinking inside that box.
            Characters Malcolm Tucker and Hugh Abbott discuss a colleague.
            Dialogue from the BBC Comedy – *The Thick of It*

In the previous chapter, we discussed how it's possible to creatively train individuals to help them deal with change. Coping strategies invariably require an individual to adopt a creative and critical approach to their situation since the behaviour that they've always adopted will no longer give them the results they want. To adapt the often-used truism, they *can't* do what they've always done, and so they won't *get* what they've always got.

In their day-to-day existences, though, often people are not required to think deeply about what they are doing. Creativity can come from moments of inspiration and flashes of brilliance, but it is often rare for people, especially those who are outside of the so-called 'creative' industries, to actually sit down and think about things deeply. Even in my previous incarnation as a doctoral research scientist, a field where original thought is supposedly prized above all else, I don't remember doing a great deal of isolated thinking. I read, I analyzed, I planned, I critiqued, but none of these are quite the same as having purely creative thoughts.

The analysis of data will not, in itself, produce new ideas.

Edward de Bono (Thinker)

Fortunately for the trainer, there are a huge number of books full of creativity exercises (Michael Michalko's *Thinkertoys* (2006), and Brian Clegg and Paul Birch's *Crash Course in Creativity* (2002) being two that I turn to when I need inspiration). This chapter will provide some exercises of this nature, but it will also ask you to consider whether creativity can be taught at all, how the trainer might facilitate the development of creative individuals and how simple interventions can have a major impact.

Creative Beginnings

Few people think more than two or three times a year I have made an international reputation for myself by thinking once or twice a week.

George Bernard Shaw (Playwright)

Our brains are hard-wired to use an automatic, subconscious classification system based on past experiences. When we receive new information we simply classify it and interpret it according to what we have experienced or seen before. Edward de Bono (see his classic *Lateral Thinking* (1990)) refers to this process as 'vertical' thinking; but it could also be described as 'train-line' or 'logical' processing. This gives us the competitive advantage of being able to process a huge amount of information very quickly but it also keeps us locked into current realities. The trouble with this system is that it doesn't readily allow for wholly original situations and large departures from the norm. Traditionally it was believed that in such contexts a pure and undiluted spark of creative inspiration would allow new thinking. However, as psychologists delve deeper into the topic of creativity and the lateral thought process, they are beginning to realize that the process of incubation of an idea and the surrounding classified knowledge are far more intertwined with genius than was first imagined.

A familiar illustration of how the spark of genius can apparently change the world is Sir Isaac Newton's infamous moment underneath his apple tree. Two things, however, are often omitted from this story. Firstly, Newton was the pre-eminent scientist of his (and perhaps any) age. He'd studied the sciences for his entire life. He wasn't an orchard labourer who happened to stumble on one of humankind's greatest realizations after seeing an apple drop. And secondly, the apple incident occurred some *20 years before* he announced his discovery of universal gravitation. There is clearly something more to the creative issue than simple logical processing and gradual study, but reliance on an elusive spark of inspiration is also flawed. In the interests of space, we've not provided a full run down of the major theories of creativity. If you want to know more, it's worth an examination of *How to Foster Creativity* by Simon Dewulf and Caroline Baillie (1999), and Mark Runco's *Creativity – Theories and Themes* (2007), which both provide a collection of models and materials and can provide a facilitator with a great deal of food for thought.

Can Creativity Be Taught?

As outsiders, what we often find fascinating in groups is the power of a label. Organizations have 'creative' departments, some individuals are introduced to us as being 'ideas people', and some people tell us that they're the one who 'does the thinking' in a team. These badges are purely psychological and yet can be both liberating and restrictive. Recently I was facilitating a group where a great idea came from a quiet, reticent member. Later on I lightly referred to her as being 'the creative one' and for the rest of the day the group looked to her for new ideas. At the end she revealed that she didn't think of herself as creative in the slightest, but it had been powerful to be thought of as such. So much of creativity is concerned with the beliefs which we hold about ourselves.

> *Creativity is our true nature; blocks are an unnatural thwarting of a process at once as normal and as miraculous as the blossoming of a flower at the end of a slender green stem.*
> Julia Cameron (Artist, Writer and Teacher)

So, can creativity be taught? Well, perhaps it doesn't need to be. For instance, Charlie is one of the most creative people we know. He views the world as an open book and has very few preconceptions about what the correct answer is to a problem. He constantly surprises us with his novel solutions to problems that other people think are impossible. Charlie, however, is not especially gifted in any way.

He's just a four-year-old child.

In terms of his creativity, he's not yet encumbered by the structures that formal education and life experience brings. To him, a cardboard box is a racing car, the sofa is another planet. Life simply hasn't yet told him that that's the wrong answer.

Charlie isn't special; we've all been like that. So, we'd argue that creativity doesn't need to be taught, *it needs to be reawakened, remembered and permitted.* Much of this reawakening can start with an examination of your own situation. These questions are of equal use to you personally or to your delegates and learners.

Practitioner's Enquiries

What physical conditions do you need to have in place to be creative?

What would be your perfect creative environment? How could you realistically adapt your work environment to this end?

When is your best creative time of day? Is this different from your most productive time?

How do you protect your good quality thinking time?

How do you make sure you don't lose your good ideas?

How do other people affect your creative abilities?

How do you know if an idea is a good one? Or if it has potential?

What feelings do you get if an idea is good?

Where (typically) do you have your good ideas?

Focus on this last question for a moment. Where *do* you have ideas? When you're out running? When you're in the shower? When you're half asleep? It's highly unlikely that either 'sitting in front of my computer' or 'when I'm told I must be creative' came high on your list. You may have found that physical activity promotes novel thought; it's thought this is to do with our ancestors spending a far greater proportion of their time foraging whilst walking. And so does dissociation: the good ideas come when you're thinking of something different.

Creating a Creative Environment

Look sharply after your thoughts. They come unlooked for, like a new bird seen in your trees, and, if you turn to your usual task, disappear.

Ralph Waldo Emmerson (Essayist and Poet)

So how could you as a facilitator help to create a creative environment for your delegates? What physical, mental and emotional conditions will allow people to engage with materials creatively? How could you remove distractions? How could you allow participants to focus on tackling problems in new and creative ways without being bothered by their phone, email, boss, team or life? Why not treat this as a creativity warm-up for yourself:

Practitioner's Exercise

Take each of the following words or concepts and consider three different ways that you could use each of them to help stimulate a creative environment.

Movement and Action	Music	Incubation
Quantity	Childlike	Calm
Pictures	Options	Spatial Environment
Rhythm	Energy	Lists
Colour	Celebrity	Challenge

Also, if you are facilitating an idea generation meeting, are you ensuring that you build in time and space for the resultant ideas to be captured in a portable form that can be taken back to the world outside the retreat or meeting room?

Do Organizations Want *Creative* Thinkers?

Thinking men cannot be ruled.

Ayn Rand (Writer)

In a workplace environment, it is unlikely that employees are required to be totally creative. Certainly I've worked within organizations where my creative ideas have been *too* radical and I've had to grudgingly dilute them. The originality of the idea was never in question but, with hindsight, perhaps the practicality was. Educational organizations may be slightly different in this, in that the aims here are, in theory at least, more transferable. However, the creative learning outcomes in these institutions are also restricted.

It is far more likely that what an organization wants is a force of creative *problem solvers*, who share the end goal of building or supporting the organization. So regardless of the specific theoretical creative process that you believe in, as a facilitator there are a number of unifying notions which you must embrace if your interventions are to be appropriate. Notice how similar these notions are to the principles of exercise design that we outlined in Part I of this book. The rest of the chapter will examine each in turn and provide a number of ideas and exercises that the creative trainer can use.

1	Exploring and Understanding the Goal	Much of the creative problem-solving process comes in exploring the problem, finding the *real* problem and reducing some of the logical barriers that people erect with the assumptions that they make and the words they use.
2	Real World Skills, Techniques and Knowledge	Teresa Amabile (*Creativity in Context,* 1996) points out that critical creativity can only truly be valuable if it sits on top of a sound domain framework of skills, knowledge and attitudes. This is not to say that fresh eyes are not useful, but a degree of practical understanding of the domain is essential.
3	Motivation	Wanting to solve the problem, wanting to immerse yourself in it, truly loving the area and wanting to succeed are, as Abraham Lincoln once noted 'more important than any one thing'.
4	Pure Creativity	Seeing the problem in new ways and breaking free of the logical constraints imposed because 'that's how it's always been done'. Providing or establishing an environment in which people are free to be wrong, make mistakes and challenge what is the correct way of thinking.
5	Critical Judgement	Understanding the practicality of our solutions and whether they'll be fit for purpose in reality.
6	Implementation	Having the skill and will to implement our ideas, or to 'sell' them to whoever makes the implementation decision.

Creative Component 1: Exploring and Understanding the Goal

To arrive at a creative solution to a problem we must first understand what that problem really is. This sounds trite and simplistic, but is often ignored by unfacilitated groups who think they know the dimensions of the problem already and focus all of their efforts in moving straight into finding solutions for it. However, to not fully explore the issue means that our assumptions, beliefs and word choices can lead us try and solve the 'wrong' problem.

Our creativity (and effectiveness in other departments) is limited by our persistence in holding on to the notion that our beliefs are true, our beliefs are made upon real data and the data that we select are the real data. In the book *The Fifth Discipline Fieldbook: Strategies for Building a Learning Organization*, Peter Senge (1994) outlines a helpful tool called the Ladder of Inference which is based on the work of (amongst others) William Isaac and Chris Argyris.

In this model they essentially state that:

Our actions are driven by our *beliefs*
Our beliefs are formed from *conclusions* that we draw
We draw conclusions from *assumptions* that we make
Our assumptions are made around the *meanings* of certain data
The data is not complete and is a small *selection* of the whole picture

Understanding the Goal Exercise – 'Off the Floor'

I sometimes demonstrate this notion by using an adaptation of an old exercise wherein I arrange a group into a circle and place a sheet of paper in front of each of them. I ask them to imagine that they are in a field with no furniture and explain that the sheet represents a barrier* between their feet and the floor. I then ask them to be 'off the floor' and one or two of them will step onto their paper. Such is the power of the way that human beings conform (labelled 'groupthink' by psychologist Irving Janis) that the rest of the group will follow this lead. I'll ask the group to 'reset' and they'll step back on to the carpet. I reinforce the command-response pattern by repeating the 'off the floor' and 'reset' statements. The 'reset' is a deliberate word choice, and is deliberately selected so as not to invalidate the point of the exercise. Once the group are conditioned to accept the paper as *the* solution for the problem, I'll remove some of the papers. The instruction 'be off the floor' is now greeted by a clamour of group members trying to share each other's paper and holding on tightly to each other to retain balance. The more paper that gets removed, the more the group find it difficult to 'be off the floor' until only one sheet remains and the problem is nearly impossible to solve.

The key to the learning point is to stop the group and give them time to consider the question,

'What precisely and specifically is the problem here?'

Of course, they may answer in the following ways: 'The paper is too small' or 'There are too many of us' or 'We don't feel comfortable holding on to each other and we can't balance without doing so.'

However, none of these are the 'right' problems. They're just self-constructed barriers based on the method that they've chosen to solve the problem. I've provided a (not 'the') tool, which then gets removed. Their logical thought processing (and groupthink) combined with my reinforcement of a workable tool leads them to believe the paper must be the right solution, and stops them revisiting the real problem which is

'be off the floor'.

Any beliefs about the task concerning 'for a period of time', 'using the paper' or 'until the trainer says otherwise' (hence 'reset') are based on inferred assumption only. A simultaneous one centimetre jump into the air from each individual would solve the problem as stated. The difficulties come from assumptions.

Note: * Not '*the* barrier', but '*a* barrier'.

Helping groups or individuals to consider what assumptions they are making is hugely powerful in breaking an established pattern of thoughts. And of course, the ladder starts to loop and self-perpetuate because the data that we collect in the future is subjective, based on our current belief. Also consider how useful this type of thinking could be in helping individuals to converse well with each other (Chapter 9) or understanding diversity issues (Chapter 10).

Beliefs Exercise – Tangram Treachery

I had this idea a long time ago as an office prank for a puzzle-loving colleague, and then realized how useful it could be as an exercise.* The task, which was inspired by the Tangram (an ancient Chinese puzzle which uses seven pieces which combine to form a perfect square), can be used to very quickly highlight the assumptions that we make when tackling problems.

Kit required: Blank A4 paper or card and scissors.

Time: It takes as long as you let it. We recommend no more than ten minutes.

People: One set of shapes per two to four people in small groups.

Take a piece of plain rectangular paper, mark it out and cut it into 10–15 pieces which are geometrically regular and more or less equally sized, as illustrated in Figure 7.1. Do a quick sketch of the pattern you create, so that you can reveal the answer later on.

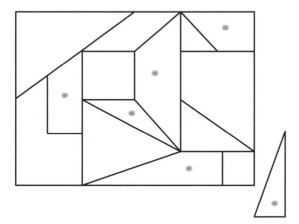

Figure 7.1   Equipment set-up for 'Tangram Treachery' exercise

Then, from an identical piece of paper or card, cut another similarly sized and shaped piece (as illustrated above).

Shuffle all the pieces together and turn some over. Place a small dot in the centre of all of them; in the illustration, some of the dots are hidden on the back of the shapes. Shuffle the shapes again and turn some over, so some spots are up and some down.

Hand the bundle of shapes to the group and ask the group to, without overlapping any pieces, reform the piece of A4 paper. Provide no further clarifications, and certainly don't precede the task by telling a group that this task is about testing assumptions.

Of course, if the group assumes (because of familiarity of the Tangram form) that all the pieces must be used then this is impossible – but this won't stop some of them trying almost indefinitely. The point here is to watch for and listen to their assumptions.

Do they believe that all the pieces must be used? Do they believe that all the dots must be face up? Do they believe that it 'must be possible'? Notice how quickly they move to try and form the sides or corners, rather than thinking the task through.

As a short exercise, in some ways it is a very cheap trick. It does, however, make enormously powerful points about assumptions and the way we approach problems where the solution is obvious. Ensure that these lessons are drawn out in review, and promise the group that there won't be any further devious cheats of this nature for the remainder of the session.

Note: * Subsequent to the creation of this exercise, there have been professionally-produced activities which use similar principles. See Challenging Assumptions at http://www.rsvpdesign.co.uk/.

Of course, assumptions can be captured and challenged with far more realistic activities and with far less treachery than in the previous exercise. For example, providing a group with a nebulous or very broad aim means that assumptions are necessary to make any headway whatsoever. Such a nebulous and broad goal is provided in this next exercise suggestion.

Understanding the Goal Exercise – Rubbish Training

Kit required: Household recycling junk (plastic pots, cardboard tubes and so on), stationery, scissors and tape.

People: Kit dependent. Groups of four to six people for each set of kit.

Time required: Anywhere between 15 minutes and three hours.

Provide each group with a large amount of household junk and stationery and ask them to:

Using the materials provided create a training exercise that will help other groups to learn about different aspects of workplace effectiveness.

(As a trainer, think for just one minute about how *you* would tackle the exercise. Now stop and list the assumptions you've already made. There'll be hundreds. Each of these is leading you to directions that may be fruitful, or may not.)

After five minutes, ask the group to pause their activity and to list on a flipchart all the assumptions that they have *already* made about training, effectiveness, workplace and so on.

The exercise could stop at this point and lead into discussions around decision-making and assumptions, but is better if it continues with the manufacture of training exercises.

This may sound in some ways like the ultimate trainer's indulgence, but asking a group to collectively go through the process that we described in Part I of this book will require that they be creative *and* consider a different facet of their workplace effectiveness.

Given sufficient time you could then have another sub-group undertake the training exercise that the first group created. Due to time constraints, this second part of the exercise may not work as well as you may wish it to (as an actual workable solution may take far longer to create than a describable but incomplete activity). Regardless of how practical a group's solution is, it can provide powerful future inspiration for the resourceful trainer.

Any topic will work with an exercise such as this provided that the given brief is suitably nebulous to allow the group to explore the problem properly. Often 'creativity' sessions don't facilitate the exploration of ideas well enough, meaning that groups or individuals quickly brainstorm and then select the least bad of their first three ideas.

CREATIVE QUESTIONS WITH POWER

In addition to the assumptions that we make, our creativity is often limited by the words that we use to explore a problem. As consultants, we both often sit in meetings with clients who want to know how to solve a certain problem. For instance, they may want ideas around increasing their training programme's reach in an organization. We find that the creative juices flow much more readily if a problem is stated as a *precise* question, and we'll often ask them something like, 'What's the specific question we're talking about here?' Often the resultant question will be surprising and will add a huge degree of colour to the issue. They might say, for example, 'How can we convince our managers to release their teams to attend training?' – which is a very different agenda to the one they initially stated. The power of the question here is that asking it starts to affect the parameters of the problem at hand. Also, it can start our own innate curiosity flowing in a way that a straight issue doesn't.

Practitioner's Exercise (a)

Think about a problem that you face in your professional life. Write it down as a bullet point. Now craft it as a precise and specific question, which is grammatically and semantically correct.

Think about how you feel when you examine the bullet point and the question separately.

DIFFERENT WORDS, DIFFERENT PROBLEMS

As mentioned above, words are very powerful forces when it comes to shaping our understanding of a problem and therefore in processing that problem to generate a workable solution. In order to examine a problem more creatively, it's worth playing with the question, or 'reframing' it. To return to the illustrative conversation about recruiting people to training courses, the client's question, 'How can we convince our managers to release their teams to attend training?' could be reframed as:

'What might entice our leaders to develop their people?' *or*
'How could we make our product irresistible to our decision-makers?' *or*
'What gets in the way of our supervisors allowing their teams to improve?'

All of these questions are potentially very different solution generators.

Practitioner's Exercise (b)

Go back to your question from part (a) above. Now rewrite the problem in at least three different ways. Don't use leading questions; ensure you stay in questioning form *and use completely different words* each time.

Now think about how each of the different questions makes you feel, and what thoughts you have, as you examine each of the options.

Reframing can be a neat and profound way of having a group learn to explore a problem more fully before they try to solve it.

Exercise Ideas – Exploring and Reframing

You could run the above Practitioner's Exercise with a group in its current form. Alternatively you could set them a real problem from the workplace and ask them to go through the described process in a small group.

Alternatively you could set up a learning group of four or more people. Issue each group member with a piece of paper with four boxes, numbered one to four. Ask each member of the group to write a real-life work issue into the first box of their paper in question form.

Then introduce the notion of restating the problem using new words. Ask them to reframe their own problem using entirely new words and write it in box number two. Stress that they mustn't solve the problem, just play with the question.

Then have them pass their paper clockwise one place around the group, and then ask each member to provide a creative reframe *for their neighbour's problem* in box three. Then have the paper folded and sent back to the start position.

Then repeat, only with the paper being passed to their anticlockwise neighbour. Before this final iteration it may be worth mentioning to the group about what a powerful question is (see Part II of this book, in the section entitled 'Strategy 5: *Ask Fewer, More Powerful Questions'*, page 34, for a reminder).

When the exercise is complete, have each person discuss their thoughts and reactions with the person opposite, who has not contributed anything in the previous two rounds.

Understanding a problem, so as to solve it better creatively, is as much about having the time, space and freedom to play with it, free of constraints and strictures, as anything else. As facilitators, the central question to ask ourselves is this: 'How can we encourage our people to be more childlike (though not childish) in the way they tackle their thoughts?'

CREATIVITY AT DIFFERENT LEVELS

I was in a supermarket the other day, and I heard the following conversation between a parent and his young child:

'Shall we buy some apples?' the father said. 'Why?' replied the child. 'Because they're good for us,' the father stated, his tone rich with scientific confidence. 'Why?' questioned his progeny. 'Er...'cause they've got vitamins!' the father replied though I could hear definite hesitancy before he answered. And then the child played his trump card: 'Why?'

At this point I looked at the father to see how he handled the question. All I could see in his eyes was fear and bewilderment, as he processed the enquiry, 'Why *do* apples have vitamins?' (Isn't that a brilliant question? I've a bioscience PhD and I never asked a question that good in all my time at university.) His answer was to adopt the tactic that my parents once adopted and the same one that I'll no doubt adopt with my children: 'Look, we're just going to get some apples. OK? And some bananas.'

In their book *Tools for Dreamers*, Robert Dilts et al. (1991) refer to this style of enquiry as chunking, that is, exploring a problem by examining it at different levels (or chunks) of information.

Asking 'Why is that a problem?' places the focus of the question upwards towards the metaphysical big picture. Conversely, asking the question, 'What's a part of that problem?' places the focus downwards on to the specific details of the issue. Both of these types of questions can be difficult to answer.

The movement towards less-abstract objectives and more specific problems will help to focus a session from simple idea exploration onto the skills, techniques and knowledge that the participants bring from the 'real world'.

Good judgement comes from experience, and often experience comes from bad judgement.
Rita Mae Brown (American Writer)

Creative Chunking – Exercise Idea

Prepare a bag full of random objects and representative concepts (as per suggestions below) and a coin.

Pen	Wristwatch (Time)	Sock	Religious Icon (Religion)	Screwdriver
Medal (Recognition)	Cup	Diary (Work)	Dice	Perfume (Beauty)
Toothbrush	Fork (Eat)	Toy Car	Passport (Travel)	Tea Bag

Participants flip the coin: heads means 'chunk up' and tails means 'chunk down'. Participants take an object from the bag and (depending on the previous coin toss) must quickly and briefly explore the object until they can go no further either up or down.

For instance, the object is a pen and their coin landed heads for chunk up. This means the participant needs to vocally consider the *purpose* of a pen; and the *purpose* of that purpose and so on until they run out of thoughts, namely:

Pen → Writing → Communication → Sharing → Humanity → Existence

For instance, if the object is a ticket (annotated with the word 'entertainment') and they threw a tail so the participant must chunk down on the detail of specific parts of that concept until they run out of thoughts, namely:

Entertainment → Film → Cinema → Popcorn → Toffee → Sugar

Once they've explored this, give them some genuine problems to explore and (continuing with the coin toss) ask them to chunk up and down until they find interesting material to play with. Suggested topics include:

How could people be more environmentally responsible?

How could we improve the community spirit of this town?

How could we improve life for all employees of this company?

Creative Component 2: Real World Skills, Techniques and Knowledge

Knowledge about the real world and the surrounding domain of the problem is not the same as critical ability and judgement about whether a solution will 'work' or not. It's about people having the right type of knowledge of their domain to approach a problem and at the same time suspending their judgement. As such, as a facilitator there is often little you can do in this regard, since your areas of expertise may differ hugely. However, an area in which an outsider *can* contribute is in helping the groups establish a workable creative process.

In the book *The Art of Innovation,* Tom Kelley (2001) describes the brainstorming process which his creative consultancy go through in order to achieve consistently creative results. The limitations and parameters that they place on phases of idea generation are all rigorously monitored. This sounds at odds with the creative process, but works well for his team and organization. So what could you do to help a team to create the best creative process for them? The practitioner questions at the beginning of this chapter would be a good place to start.

WHAT *DON'T* YOU WANT?

Elsewhere in this book we've explored at length the notion of goal-setting and how to help learners to add structure to their personal effectiveness goals. In any sort of critical creative process it's worth revisiting this notion as an issue moves from the exploratory domain and into real world consideration.

> *In whatever position you find yourself, first determine your objective.*
> Marshal Ferdinand Foch (World War One Commander)

Generally, people would agree with the sense in firming up a goal before you start to explore, but, as a note of caution, it is always worth listening to the tone adopted by groups as they start to firm up their problem-solving state. For instance, a few months ago I was working in a consultative role with an administrative team on an away day. The new team leader was chairing a discussion about the future strategy of the unit, and to start the conversation wrote on the flipchart, 'Where do we want to go?' The team looked on in silence. Eventually one of them spoke. 'Well...I'm not sure, but I don't want to revisit the problems we've had this year.' There was general agreement with this assertion. 'Me neither,' said a colleague. 'And can we have a solution that doesn't mean we have to process everything three times?' Notice how quickly the open frame of the enquiry turned into two negative positions. The team didn't know what they wanted, just what they *didn't* want, which is not the same thing at all.

For groups to be constructive in their goal-setting (or 'Beginning with the End in Mind' as we referred to in Chapter 5), rather than blindly moving away from an undesirable state, can be a huge wrench for them. As a facilitator you can have an enormous influence on the creativity of a group by noticing the way that they explore problems and helping them to be both positive and precise in their enquiries.

A final way in which the real domain can be of use in the critical creative process is in the parallel worlds of similar, but different experiences. Stopping a group and asking them, 'Where have you experienced a problem like this before?' and helping them to tease out the transferable learning from those past episodes can be your most valuable intervention.

Another way in which the real world domain creeps into the creative process is by the imposition of rules. Sometimes these can be creatively helpful; for instance, how would you paint the world if you could only use blue paint? On the face of things such a constraint seems very limiting; however to realize the full creative potential of such a restriction look at what Picasso produced in his Blue Period at the start of the twentieth century. If the rule is deliberately chosen to help the creative process, this is different to an overlooked assumption.

Real world rules can be simulated in artificial creative interventions. Take for example the following creativity warm-up exercise.

Creativity Exercise Idea – Totally Useless

Present the group with a totally useless combination of items that would be impractical and apparently useless in combination. If you actually hand out the pairs of objects, this is even better.

Ice Saucepan	Biscuit T-Shirt	Toothpaste Mallet
Chocolate Teapot	Balloon Dartboard	Water Sticky Tape

Ask them to brainstorm possible uses of these items in combination.

The twist on a normal creativity warm-up is to discreetly ask different groups to tackle their problem in different ways (to simulate real world rules). For instance:

Ask group W to find 20 uses in five minutes.

Ask group X to find 50 uses in five minutes.

Ask group Y to find as many uses as they can in five minutes.

Ask group Z to find as many uses as they can (with no time constraint applied, but stop them after five minutes).

Debrief around whether the way a question is posed affects the way it's approached. Expand this discussion to rules and conditions to the way that teams are asked to problem solve in reality and whether this is as helpful as it could be.

If you want a good idea, get lots of ideas.

Linus Pauling (Nobel Laureate)

Creative Component 3: Motivation

Having the processing tools and the mental aptitude to explore a problem is not the same as actually *wanting* to solve the problem at hand. To paraphrase Lincoln again, much, if not most, of successful critical creativity comes from someone wanting to immerse themselves in a problem, truly loving the area and wanting to succeed. Great leaps in thought come from people who have lived and breathed a question for years, and such perseverance requires motivation.

Yet in a boardroom, training room or classroom, where artificial problems are used to stimulate a group, this can be forgotten. This approach can work superficially, due to group pressures and short-term interest, but it's not the same as eliciting and using a real problem.

Practitioner's Enquiry

How could you encourage participants to share real issues and problems and use these as sample materials in a creativity intervention?

An elegant solution is to pose a nebulous and challenging question to the group by email a week or so before you are due to be meeting. Don't ask for onerous reports or presentations, but request that they go to a place where they can be creative, and think for an hour. This incubation can be hugely powerful, both because of the cognitive processing it requires, and the behavioural change of moving physical location. As a facilitator, pay attention to how often a group's incubation period is interrupted by premature criticism or implementation.

The most beautiful thing in the world is, precisely, the conjunction of learning and inspiration. Oh, the passion for research and the joy of discovery!

Wanda Landowska (Musician)

Exercise Idea – Totally Useless Revisited

To illustrate how to build momentum from one task to another (each with a discrete learning point), we have revisited the previous exercise idea.

Exercise One: 'Totally Useless' brainstorm.

Exercise Two: Clarify and select one of the ideas from stage one and build it using materials salvageable within a 100 metre radius.

Exercise Three: Create a novel and polished 'Dragon's Den'-style pitch to ask for funding for the fictitious enterprise.

Exercise Four: Design a novel advertising strategy and field-test the resulting marketing materials.

This sequence could be used with a 'business game' focus, or with a purely creative end-product. Think also what other skills and knowledge such a programme of activity could build (if properly explored and reviewed).

As a caveat here, you should be prepared for the possibility that the group rebel, or that their solution in Exercise One is unviable to see through to the end. What do you have in reserve in the event of such possibilities?

Linking exercises and activities, so the end product of one creative process becomes the starting point for the next, can be helpful in building motivation and investment from the group.

Regardless of the types learning experiences that you choose, you should acknowledge that for the exercise to be transferable it should simulate the conditions (if not the topic) that the learners would be exposed to in reality.

Genius is one per cent inspiration, ninety-nine per cent perspiration.

Thomas Edison (Inventor)

Creative Component 4: Pure Creativity

Every child is an artist. The problem is how to remain an artist once we grow up.

Pablo Picasso (Artist)

There are thousands of creativity techniques, but many of them can be reduced to sit under one or two umbrella classifications. Once the problem has been explored, reframed and processed and existing solutions from real situations have been exhausted, and artificial rules and constraints have been applied, we find that there are two main areas that creativity tends to come from. Firstly, applying positive constraints that channel the enquiry and thus giving it momentum and energy; and secondly, finding associations between unconnected items (or seeing something that is obvious to you but no one else sees). To grow an ability to think in these ways requires practice and a certain amount of playfulness.

THE POWER OF 'WHAT IF...?'

People who are purely creative open up the issues. They process divergently and ask, 'What if I did this...?' or, 'What *might* I do here?' People who are purely productive tend to do the convergent opposite and ask, 'What *must* I do by when?' Creative problem solvers do both.

Exercise Idea – 'What If?' Mixer

This exercise works best with higher numbers of people. Using sticky notes, create a series of 'What if?' question cards. Each card should contain one hypothetical question such as:

What if we all had six fingers on each hand?

What if owls drove buses?

What if the sky appeared green?

What if air cost money?

What if insects produced petrol?

What if there was no friction?

What if all communication was musical?

What if the fork hadn't been invented?

What if we were ruled by cartoon characters?

What if water was like jelly?

Distribute one card to each participant, and have the whole group mingle. At the sound of a bell or whistle, participants should talk to the person nearest to them for two minutes. In this time they should ask their 'What if?' question to their new friend who has to reply, 'That would be fantastic because...' at least five times in their minute. Then they ask *their* question to the first person. The *positive framing* of the answer is an important rule, as it stops any critical response before it has a chance to take hold. After two minutes, blow the whistle and move them on to their next partner who has a new question waiting for them. Repeat the two minute cycle three, four or five times.

What is interesting after the exercise is to ask the group how they found it, as they will almost certainly find the process gets easier with each round. The noise in the room will have increased too!

If your learners are to see the possibilities in situations then, as a key tool, 'what' and 'if' when used in combination are perhaps the two most powerful words they will ever have.

Asking 'What if?' questions of a group and encouraging them to do likewise is a very useful creative tool, and it can have even greater impact if the subject matter is real.

Exercise Idea – 'What If?' In Reality

Ask groups to identify a problem in the world around them. For instance, I'm writing this part of the chapter whilst travelling on a train and I've just had to stand in the buffet car for nearly 20 minutes, waiting to be served. The problem here might be 'How could the on-board catering be more effective?'

Have the group write the question on a flipchart or whiteboard and then for five minutes all individually write relevant 'What if?' questions (and only questions) on to sticky notes.

When five minutes have elapsed, ask each group member to stick their questions to the board and facilitate a discussion around how that creative process felt and which questions provide the most scope for exploration.

Then, ask the team to group the questions according to type. Some will be process-linked (transferable) questions and some will be task-focused (special case) questions:

Process (transferable)	Task (special case)
What if the solution had to be done by tomorrow?	What if hot food came to you instead of vice versa?
What if the solution had to be free?	What if there were lots of small buffets instead of one large one?
What if we could change people's perceptions?	What if you could pre-order your food when you bought your ticket?
What if we had infinite/time money?	What if there was no on-board buffet at all?
What if the solution was impossible?	What if there was a limit on the number of items purchased?
What if we looked for the answer in another environment?	What if only one person could queue?

Compile the process questions, and discuss how useful these would be as a transferable creative aid away from this meeting.

'WHAT IF...' WE DID THE WRONG THING?

When I'm blocked, I often find that inverting the problem and thinking about the 'wrong answer' is far more fun, and in addition, my subconscious will then go to work on the problem on my behalf. This process of creative inversion can make a neat little warm-up exercise in which you challenge groups to make the worst solution desirable, for instance;

What's worst way to make a cup of tea?
What's the worst way to be an employee at this company?
What would be the worst way to write an essay?

Don't worry about the how sensible your questions sound – playfulness is an essential ingredient in the creative process.

Discovery consists in seeing what everyone else has seen and thinking what no-one else has thought.

Albert von Szent-Gyorgyi (Nobel Laureate)

ASSOCIATING IDEAS

The second major creative theme is concerned with finding associations, patterns and connections in things that appear unconnected. Like any other skill, this is one that can be practiced and it's certainly easy to get groups and individuals to think in associative ways.

Exercise Idea – '...Like a Fish Needs a Bicycle'

As the saying goes, 'X needs Y like a fish needs a bicycle.' So why *might* a fish need a bicycle? Challenge the group to consider it as a statement. Ask them in small groups to come up with 50 different answers in ten minutes. Alternative improbable pairings might include:

Fish Bicycle	Mole Parachute	Cat Boomerang
Worm Gloves	Cow Whisk	Goat Lawnmower

Mid-way through, pause the activity and introduce the notion of the 'What if?' question as described in the exercises above. Restart the exercise. Ask them to reflect on what happened throughout the ten minutes. The following questions may come in helpful:

How did the individuals find the free-association required by the task?

What might be the value of the ability to link ideas in reality?

What was the effect of being asked to provide 50 ideas?

Did the flow of ideas lull and pick up again?

What effect did the 'What if?' intervention have?

How might groups or individuals be able to use this new insight?

Exercise Idea – Make *This* the Answer

Have participants draw up a positive and precise question (with reframing if desired) and to write up that question on a piece of paper. Hand round a bag of household objects (tea strainer, TV remote, flask, mouse mat and so on) and ask the participants to select an object without looking in the bag. Give them three minutes to answer the question using the object and only the object. This could be a metaphorical solution ('the tea strainer sifts the nice from the unpleasant, and so I need to prioritize my tasks more effectively') or a real one ('I need to remember to take regular breaks').

Exercise Idea – How Would *They* Do It?

Search the Internet or celebrity magazines for some large photos or images of well-known historical and contemporary figures from all walks of life (for example, Margaret Thatcher, Wayne Rooney, Marie Curie, Charlie Chaplin) and stick them around the walls of the whole perimeter of the room. Pose a problem to the group (or select one from them) and ask the group to pair up and walk around the room, ensuring that they take in all of the images. When they reach an image they should stop and have a one-minute conversation about how that person would go about tackling the problem.

In free-association exercises like the two above and one below (the second two inspired by Edward de Bono's *How to be More Interesting* (1997)), learners are being asked to take a random injection into their thought process, and channel it, both building their associative powers of linking two separate ideas and perhaps unlocking answers that their subconscious knows but their conscious doesn't.

A final corollary from the last exercise is the value of the opportunities given by the combination of props and learner movement. For example, many managers and teachers are familiar with Edward de Bono's technique of Thinking Hats (2000) (if you haven't read it, go and buy *Six Thinking Hats* today), where a different metaphorical coloured hat represents a different facet of our intellectual process. Through the analogy of coloured hats, de Bono describes how a decision can be made by viewing the problem in six different ways. Sometimes this isolated labelling can be somewhat misused: I've certainly been present in a meeting where a manager has *demanded* 'some yellow hat thinking.'

Exercise Idea – Different Thoughts in Different Places

To help learners isolate their different thought processes, set up stations around the room and then pose a general question to the group as whole. Blow a whistle and have pairs or threes move to a station and tackle the question for two minutes with only a certain style of thinking (de Bono's or other – for instance, Opposite, Provocative, Emotive, Realistic, Factual, Positive, Negative, Associative, Chunked, and so on) and where they must put on different coloured party hats, T-Shirts or accessorize in an appropriate manner. Blow a whistle and request that everyone moves clockwise one station around the room. They spend another two minutes there, thinking differently and differently attired. After everyone has completed a circuit, give the groups a few minutes to bring all of their thinking together into a 'best' solution.

When debriefing this style of exercise, it is worth asking groups collectively what types of thought generated the ultimate 'best' answer. Ask them to compare and contrast this with the way that they critically solve problems in the workplace normally. Also, ask individuals at which thinking station they felt most and least comfortable, and what they might take away from this experience so as to change and optimize their thinking back in their daily life.

Creative Component 5: Critical Judgement

Much of the value in encouraging people to be creative can be undone by the degree to which they reject a seemingly 'bad' idea. In their excellent book *What if? How to Start a Creative Revolution at Work*, Dave Allan and his co-authors (1999) refer to the aforementioned exploration and incubation process as 'greenhousing' and make the point that criticism and premature judgement will shatter the greenhouse as effectively as a well-tossed stone.

If you want creative and critical thinkers in your organization, it is important that they learn to suspend their judgement and not to reject any idea too quickly. Even an apparently poor idea can often be adapted to function perfectly well.

In many organizations and teams, critical judgement and ability is highly prized, but what is often missing is the preceding notion of 'constructive' to make the criticism valuable. This can be an extremely difficult cultural shift to facilitate.

We find it useful to get teams thinking along the lines of, 'How could we make this better?' rather than, 'What's wrong with this idea?' and so any innate criticism is focused in a purely constructive and not destructive way. However, suspending judgement can easily become 'not challenging the established process' and so it can be interesting to experientially compare these differences.

Exercise Idea – So Good it's Bad/So Bad it's Good

Provide groups with an entity or organization that is widely known to be a 'good thing'. Ask them to creatively think of multiple reasons why it is purely a force for bad in the world. For instance:

Charity is completely bad because…

The United Nations is an utterly bad thing because…

This can be inverted, and the process repeated:

Pollution is wholly good because…

Tyranny is purely good because…

Or alternatively using a neutral topic (technology, progress) and having different groups focus on the good or the bad within it.

If a key element of critically creative problem-solving is to suspend judgement of an idea, then equally, at some point, thinkers need to decide whether or not an idea is sound and actually move towards implementing it.

A hunch is creativity trying to tell you something.

Frank Capra (Film Director)

JUDGING AND EVALUATING SOLUTIONS

There are various ways and means to help judge an idea, and so help teams decide whether it has mileage and how it can be improved. SWOT analysis, Forced Pair comparisons and even Kurt Lewin's ForceField analysis are among many here that can be used. Many of the tools and techniques that we suggested in Part II to help get at the honesty in a group can also be utilized here. Personally, I find that one of the most powerful enquiries that you can make in this area is whether a decision and judgement is being made with the rational head or with the emotive heart. For instance, when a friend gives me some good advice I know that they're giving me the 'right' answer. I still don't follow that advice because it's not what I *want* to do. My heart overrules my head. There is a place for both in idea evaluation, but it needs to be a conscious decision.

The creative trainer can find interesting developmental material in the way individuals choose to criticize and evaluate their own ideas.

INSPIRATION, REALISM AND CRITICISM

The interfaces between different parts of the creative process from idea to implementation are fascinating. As a facilitator, you may pick up on these and want to explore them with your group. For instance, how much time does a group spend exploring the problem and coming up with ideas, as opposed to critiquing the idea or working out how that idea would be implemented?

In his book *Strategies Of Genius: Volume I*, Robert Dilts (1994) presents a modelled process based on a number of creative thinkers, but especially that of Walt Disney. He outlines a very accessible triangular pathway of thought that moves from the purely creative *dreamer*, to a practical implementing *realist* and finally to a judgemental *critic*.

	In a Nutshell	Purpose	Helpful Transitions	Unhelpful Transition
The Dreaming Phase	'What if...?'	Not concerned with what is practical. Needs to be isolated from the other phases to create as many ideas as possible and select the ones with the most potential.	To realism after due incubation	Straight to critical
The Realistic Phase	'How could that *work*...?	The aim of the realist is to create a specific and practical solution.	Either direction	
The Critical Phase	'That won't work because...'	The aim of the critic is to find all the possible problems. This can take the form of both positive and negative evaluations.	To realism or dreaming	

If the creative process is to be effective, ideas can cycle back from the critical phase to the realistic or dreaming phase for more input. Interactions between the phases are productive (given due incubation) but moving straight from the dreaming phase to the critical is a sure way to destroy creative ideas.

Practitioner's Enquiry

How does your creative cycle work?

Can you articulate how your creative process takes a problem, explores and forms ideas, thinks realistically and then appraises the possible solutions?

Can you draw the pathway as a diagram?

What are the directions of your transitions?

Typically how much time do you spend in each phase relative to the others?

Based on your answers to the previous questions, what would you need to *do* to optimize your critically creative abilities?

These questions and the modelled process that they help describe can be used as the basis of a group exercise.

Exercise Idea – Creative and Critical Quantities

In small working parties, have the group explore a challenge from their own workplace. Ask them to act as consultants and simply to find 'creative solutions' to the problem for a fixed amount of time. Keep a score of all the statements that the group make that are wholly creative (blue), wholly realistic (green) and wholly critical (red). Each time the group make a relevant statement, place a milk-bottle top or counter of the appropriate colour on to their table, but say nothing. The group may be able to guess what the counters represent, or may ask. Say nothing. Also, note every time a creative idea gets criticized without due incubation or entering the realism phase.

At the end of the discussion, once they have presented a creative solution, explain the significance of the counters, and outline the model from which the scoring was derived. Lead a discussion around how the thinking in the group could be tuned so that ideas are properly incubated and realistically criticized.

Creative Component 6: Implementation

You know, I have one simple request. And that is to have sharks with frickin' laser beams attached to their heads. Now evidently my cycloptic colleague informs me that that can't be done. Ah, can you remind me what I pay you people for? Honestly, throw me a bone here.
      Dr Evil berates his minions in *Austin Powers: International Man of Mystery*

If an idea is to add value to an organization, it needs to be actionable. Any idea is possible to implement providing infinite time and resources are available. Workplaces, unfortunately, are not blessed with the luxury of either of those. The harsh realities of life inside an organization mean that often what is required as a product of creative meetings is not the *right* answer but the *right now* answer.

Quality exploration, motivation, incubation and constructively critical evaluation can act as a fantastic framework in which pure creativity in the meeting room can rest, but even these are no guarantee that a solution will work on the shop floor. As a facilitator, ensuring that idea generation sessions wind down with plenty of space to help groups turn their sketches, maps, collages and ideas into implementable schemes is almost as important as having the creative conversation in the first place. It is also very useful to close down with clear decisions about what actions are going to be taken, by whom and by when, to follow up the meeting or training.

Creative training exercises and games generally fall into one of two groups. Firstly, there are those exercises that have a nebulous goal and a very clear solution method (for example, brainstorm ways to use this specific kit to change the world). Secondly, there is the 'Great Egg Race'[1]/'Scrapheap Challenge' type of puzzle where the goal is very clear (get X to Y under certain conditions) but the method is unclear.

In reality, there is a third type of challenge, which is where the goal and method of solution are unknown, and the current state is a bit cloudy too. This messiness is not easy to quickly simulate but by providing learners with reviewed experiences in both of the first two groups you may leave them in a much better state to creatively deal with the issues and changes that the world can throw at them, even when they don't fully understand their current situation.

Finally, there is a massive difference between having an idea, understanding how it could be implemented and being able to convince an organizational decision maker or a superior of its worth. To do that more effectively, individuals need to understand how an organization steers a course and how it builds and maintains a quality output of product or service. Understanding organizational quality is the focus of the next chapter.

---

1   A beloved BBC TV series from my youth in which teams had to use outlandish inventions to transport eggs over various terrains.

8 *Understanding Organizational Quality*

Quality is never an accident; it is always the result of intelligent effort.
John Ruskin (Writer and Critic)

An efficiency consultant spends the day watching two municipal employees. All day long the consultant watches as one worker digs a small hole in the ground while the other watches. Then the second fills the same hole in again while the first employee watches. This pattern is repeated many times over the course of the day. Eventually the consultant can contain his frustration no longer. 'Do you not realize how ridiculous and inefficient this is?' he exclaims. 'Of course,' says one of the employees, 'but the guy who plants the seeds is on holiday.'

This is of course a very old joke, but it does highlight a very real problem in organizations, especially ones with a high degree of specialism. As the pace of change, especially that driven by technology, increases, so it is that workers, far from increasing their flexibility, are often required to fill highly specialized niche slots within the organization. We both work a great deal with large organizations, and we're both frequently staggered by how little strategic knowledge or even big-picture understanding some coalface employees have.

When this book was conceived we planned that there would be a chapter on 'Understanding the Organization' and another on 'Quality'. Yet as the book took shape we realized that to all intents and purposes they are essentially the same thing. Organizations can only really get to grips with a unilateral quality output if all contributors understand more effectively how they fit together and what each area really contributes overall. As such, both agendas are dealt with here, separately at first; though with increasing synergy.

You can accomplish anything in life, provided that you don't mind who gets the credit.
Harry S. Truman (US President)

Seeing the Bigger Picture

Time and again, management theory tells us that organizations which survive and thrive (and are the types of organizations that employees actively seek recruitment to) are the ones where the values of all parts of the organization are aligned. It can therefore be extrapolated that quality (and so success) in an organization might be linked with how well each and every single part of the machine understands its place and not only what the machine is for, but what all the other components do and how the components link.

This is not to say that modern organizations should operate by playing some sort of corporate total football (a tactical school best embodied by the Dutch side of the 1970s, in which every outfield player could take the place of any other), but it does mean that there is sometimes real benefit in having any employee understand more effectively how their organization truly operates.

To illustrate this notion, we sometimes use a learning experience wherein a group of individuals is split into three sub-groups.

- Sub-group one takes the role of the *Senior Management Team*, and is taken into a breakout room wherein they have a brief for a dynamic and changeable task, a walkie-talkie, and flipchart and pens.
- Sub-group two is taken to a different part of the building where they are furnished with a walkie-talkie attached to the table, and an instruction that they are the *Middle Management* and should wait where they are and await further instructions.
- Sub-group three represents the *Workforce* and they are given whatever kit is necessary to complete the task, but no other instructions.

On a predetermined signal the simulation will start, whereon the Senior Management will start issuing commands to the Middle Management. The Middle Management will then be required to go to the Workforce, collect information, return to their base and report back to their superiors using the walkie-talkie. The top bosses can't see what the workers are doing; the workers don't know what they should be doing; and the middle managers are caught in between. Very quickly these hierarchies become set and, while no sub-group is working optimally, none of the sub-groups challenge their roles. The bosses strategize blindly, the workers just do as they are told (because 'we're only the workers') and the poor middle managers get frustrated above and below. It's a very neat simulated experience, and I dearly wish I'd thought of it myself. However, the best part is when teams realize they can challenge the process and the senior bosses empower the workers (instead of relying on their middle management to pass a message upstairs and await a strategic decision) to respond to the dynamic changes themselves. *Yet in the dozens of times I have run exercises like this, I've only seen a group break out of their predetermined roles once – such is the power of a label.* The labels we give and take often stop us seeing the big picture, and get in the way of a quality outcome.

The conformation of an individual to the fit the stereotypes of a role that they have been given to play is well documented in psychological literature (Zimbardo's 1971 Stanford Prison experiment being probably the most notorious (Harvey et al., 1973)), but this can also apply to organizational workings too. In his book *Good to Great*, Jim Collins (2001) warns against the style of leadership which he calls 'genius with a thousand helpers'. The leader doesn't build a strong management team because he or she has no need for one, and probably doesn't want one, they just need a multitude of foot soldiers to help realize their vision. But when the genius leaves the helpers are unable to move forward. In our work, we see this situation play out a lot. As consultants we are often recruited to either facilitate the remedial action that is required when the genius departs or train a collective of talented foot soldiers who have been held back by their organization and are now required to be strategic and yet lack the experience and insight.

In strategy it is important to see distant things as if they were close and to take a distanced view of close things.

Miyamoto Musashi (Japanese Warrior and Strategist)

Understanding an organization from a trainer's perspective is helping people to:

- understand how the pieces of their organization fit together and how the connectivity works between components that may be functioning perfectly well as individual parts;
- strategically understand the environment and context in which their organization sits, why certain decisions are made and how action at a local level effects the organization as a whole and vice versa;
- build a comprehension of what real 'quality' (whether product or service) means to the organization as a whole and how each part of the organization contributes.

Practitioner's Enquiries

Think about your current organization, or organizations in which you have worked in the past.

How well do/did you really understand the workings of the organization?

How well do/did you understand what happened from start to finish insofar as the product or service was concerned?

What don't you know? What frustrates you? Which parts of the process that you cannot directly control could be more effective insofar as you are concerned?

Which decisions were made that did you not understand?

What was the ultimate goal of the organization, and how did each component contribute to that goal?

Where would it have been helpful for you to know more, and where would that knowledge have been extraneous?

How might these questions help you to design effective interventions in your trainings?

Understanding How the Pieces Fit Together

As an outsider, I often start away day-type sessions by having a group of people explain their project, team or organization to me. I do this, not because I need to know (I've usually done my homework in this regard) but because I want to see if *they* know, and whether they can explain it. I often use some sort of prop to help this process; otherwise it can sometimes result in a manager recreating the corporate organizational diagram on a flipchart, which is not what I want at all. For instance, I sometimes place poker-chips, children's building blocks or even sweets on the table and ask teams to use them to plot out their place in their organizational machine. This also works with, for example, charity teams or research teams to have them illustrate their place in a funding generation and spend stream.

The experiential element here is strengthened by challenging the group's placement of objects in relation to each other (Why is 'sales' further out from the centre of the table than 'manufacture'?) and by having the group reach consensus. What is important, and facilitated by the tactile process, is that the group discusses organization structure with regard to process, not just with regard to a corporate schematic on a wall.

Practitioner's Enquiries

Why is it really important that your learners fully understand the organization? Will it help your sales team to understand all of the research, development and manufacturing processes? What is key information and what is peripheral?

How could you allow your learners to embody the organization? What props could you use? Sweets, building blocks, action figures, beads?

What would allow them to explain the connectivity within the organization? String? Tape?

What causal factors make the processes within the organization strong, and which are the weak links? How might these strong and weak links best be embodied in a model form?

Which processes are central and which are peripheral? How might this be embodied in scale form?

How might this be captured for posterity?

To give a fully fleshed out idea to illustrate this concept, here is one that we use sometimes to have groups explore the organization in which they operate.

Understanding the Organization Exercise – House of Cards

This exercise works well with established teams, but could equally serve as part of an induction programme, provided that at least some of the group understands the organization to an extent. It works best with cross-organizational project teams who have been brought together under the banner of a strategic work package.

Time required: About 15–20 minutes, but this depends on the size of the organization, and how complex the interdepartmental links are.

Number of participants: Four to eight. More than eight, use multiple groups and build in time for them to present to each other at the end.

Kit required: A standard deck of playing cards (optionally including jokers).

It requires a large flat space, like a conference table, but a large area of flooring would also suffice. (A nice twist is to carry out the activity on a large expanse of paper and after the completion of the exercise, have the group map out the result using marker pens.)

Give the group a deck of 52 standard playing cards (and jokers). Since you are probably an outsider to the team, ask them to help you to understand the context in which they work.

Ask them to explain their organization (or school, company, sector, department and so on) with the cards as aids and to lay the cards out in the way that they see their organizational structure. What level of explanation depends on the size of the organization, but in most situations, 52(+2) cards give enough scope to explain the senior management team, the hierarchies in each department and how these interplay.

Give them 15 minutes to discuss and finalize their answer and five minutes to present it back to you.

This exercise works for a number of reasons. The humour involved in having a group decide that finance are clubs (because they beat you for money) and HR are hearts (because they're compassionate) can often act as a task opener. It can also open other potentially powerful avenues of enquiry. For instance is the CEO a queen of hearts or spades? Why? What led the team to that label?

However, building on this, the group may start to make value calls about the respective worth of a part of an organization (marketing are a 'three', whereas Research and Development are a 'nine' and so on). In addition, the task also requires that teams place the cards on a table which means that they can represent the hierarchies in the organization (what goes at the 'top'?) and also which parts of the organization are close to the centre and which are near the edge (metaphorically or literally). At times, you can query their decisions. For instance is department X *really* the same value to the organization Y as department D, and is it *really* the same distance out from the centre? Such enquiries are a great way of opening up discussions around organizational process.

In addition, asking a group to do this forces them to look outside of their own part of the organization, both 'upwards' and 'sideways', and having a cross-disciplinary project team reaching a consensus on values-based judgements of this matter can be a very powerful opener to other points.

In the previous chapters we have explored the concepts around teamwork and diversity and how an individual relates to the rules imposed by an organization, whether explicitly or implicitly within its embedded culture. Similar exercises and ideas as given in those chapters can also be adapted to have groups explore the rules and processes within an organization.

To find fault is easy; to do better may be difficult.
Plutarch (Greco-Roman Historian and Writer)

Understanding how the organization works is of course linked to an appreciation of what each part of the organization truly does. To do this effectively it may be worth to start a training intervention close to home, and consider what a group's own department actually does, and how it might improve the quality and consistency of its product or service. After all, as we explore elsewhere many times in this book (especially in Chapter 5 'Building Personal Effectiveness'), it's often much easier for someone to find fault externally than it is to truly reflect on their own shortcomings. In the spirit of this book, of piquing your creativity rather than telling you the answers, here are five ideas for how a creative training experience might give a group insight into the complex workings of an organization.

Understanding the Organization Exercise Ideas

Organization Exercise Idea One	Facilitator Notes and Thoughts
Ask the group to develop a (from first-principle) plan of a children's day care nursery centre. Their thinking should include consideration of customer focus, staffing, legislation compliance, location, marketing, approximated realistic pricing.	This type of exercise works well because the initial preconception is that it's going to be relatively easy. That it isn't and that it gets very complicated very quickly helps them to understand that even small organizations are complex, and that their own corner of a massive organization is linked to other parts of the organization even if they don't notice it on a day-to-day basis.
Organization Exercise Idea Two	**Facilitator Notes and Thoughts**
Think of an organization as a spider's web. When one part of the web is touched, vibrations are sent to all areas of the web. Have teams draw themselves at the centre of a web and ask to draw in the connections and how vibrations move outwards.	Having individuals place themselves at the centre of an organization can be enormously powerful. Usually employees might see themselves as being junior or senior, but not necessarily central. It helps the group or individual to understand synergies and connections between their work and the work of the organization as a whole.
Organization Exercise Idea Three	**Facilitator Notes and Thoughts**
Write each of the sectional, departmental or team names for the company on to individual cards. Lay them out on the table (or stick them to a corkboard) and give the groups masking tape, string, pins and sticky dots. Ask them to identify the *processes* which link the different parts of the organization.	The end result of this type of more advanced exercise can look very similar to the previous one, however, by focusing on the intradepartmental *processes*, the group or groups create a fantastic blank canvas upon which discussions regarding the quality of those processes and the effectiveness of measures such as information flow can be built.
Organization Exercise Idea Four	**Facilitator Notes and Thoughts**
Give each member of the group five sticky notes. Ask them each to list the five greatest concerns or challenges facing their department on to these five sticky notes. Stick these up on a wall or flipchart, and then move all of the duplicates to a different space around the room. So, for example, all the notes concerning 'communication' are placed in the same location. Arrange the group into cross-departmental trouble-shooting teams and have them come up with solutions to the shared problems.	This is a very real type of exercise and it works partly due to this reality, but also due to the fact that the issue or concern exists in a tangible (albeit sticky note) form. It can't be ducked or denied if it exists on the wall. Seeing that other departments have the same concerns gives teams a sense of shared purpose and ensures that any ideas that they produce are more likely to be workable as they have incorporated information and concerns from multiple sources. If ideas from this type of session can be implemented, and changes are actually effected, this can be a huge motivational force.

Organization Exercise Idea Five	Facilitator Notes and Thoughts
Ask groups to creatively speculate around a given hypothetical change that would affect the entire organization: For instance, what if the organization had to exist on a third of its current budget? What if all employees were only permitted to work in the organization for two years? What if meetings were banned?	This type of creative speculation allows groups and individuals to focus on what is essential to their organization. It encourages them to look at the root of what is important to the organizational mission – for example, would running at a third of the existing budget necessitate across-the-board pruning, or would it be more effective to cut the most expensive department, which is central to the organizational strategy? How would such a far-reaching and unilateral change *really* affect their organization?

As a creative trainer, it is important to remember that generally people *want* to improve and do their jobs more effectively. They will work more efficiently if they understand the goals, visions and workings of their organizations. In addition, if they can contribute ideas upwards then productivity and motivation can increase hugely. The review part of any exercise becomes paramount, especially if the ensuing ideas can be captured and used for real.

The organization may be able to function without this kind of understanding, but the quality of product or service will certainly be improved if each part functions in harmony with the others.

Quality: The Difference between 'Good Enough' and 'Great'

How much time within your job do you spend rectifying mistakes, looking for misplaced items, checking on late actions, or tweaking work that was hurriedly carried out in a pre-deadline panic? How many times is your product, service or work not right first time? The fact that you are conscientious is not in question, but there is a huge difference between effort, effectiveness and efficiency. How much time, money and resource are spent across your team, department or organization when you multiply these small inefficiencies?

Quality means doing it right when no one is looking.

Henry Ford (Industrialist)

By improving the quality of their outputs (product, service, general work) individuals can reduce the amount of rework that they undertake, organizations can lower costs and with increases in quality comes a better reputation and probably an increased market share (or equivalent depending upon in which sector the organization resides).

The Pareto Principle says that in many situations and scenarios roughly 80 per cent of the effects come from 20 per cent of the causes. The term was formed in the 1930s by Dr Joseph Juran, one of the great quality management thinkers, who named the concept after an Italian economist named Vilfredo Pareto. Many years before that, Pareto had realized that about 80 per cent of Italian land was owned and controlled by 20 per cent of the populace. Juran referred to the 'vital few and the trivial many' as a way of urging managers and leaders to focus on the things within their domains that provided the real returns. This rule of thumb is often quoted and used in the workplace in a '80 per cent of your profits come from 20 per cent of your sales'-type of statement. However, as true as Pareto and Juran's observations are, they can also be the corrupted source of some anti-quality thinking. Certainly in several jobs (especially in my first couple of low-wage employments) I have been told by a manager that '80 per cent is good enough' and that they 'didn't want perfection, just 80 per cent'. At the time this confused me, as I couldn't square this notion with doing a good job. However, I learned in time that sometimes 80 per cent *is* good enough and sometimes it *isn't*. After all, I wouldn't want to be operated on by a surgeon who was going to do an 'ok' job; I want 100 per cent performance in that situation. Similarly, I don't want to be flown by a pilot who safely lands only four times out of every five flights. However, I don't need a sales assistant to give 100 per cent service, packing my groceries and carrying them to my car; it is sufficient that they are courteous and accurate. Understanding of what quality is within an organization is clearly a highly complex issue, but it can be reduced to some key notions. Again, as a practitioner, try starting with your own experience.

Practitioner's Enquiries

In a workplace context, for your current employment, what would you say was 'quality'?

What level of performance would be 'good enough'?

What would be 'excellent'?

What would be 'better than excellent'?

How did you arrive at your answers to the previous questions? Was it explicitly explained to you on your first day or is it an implicit understanding throughout the organization?

Does your prime driver for a quality performance come from without or is it an internal one? Are your standards imposed on you or do you define what a quality performance is, or is it a little of both?

Think of the last time that you experienced fabulous service or had a fantastic time as a consumer. What *specifically* was it that made that experience so fantastic or fabulous? What did that organization do to or for you that made them stand out from the crowd?

How natural did that experience seem? Did the staff seem to behave in that way because they *had to* or because they *wanted to*?

The Foundations of the Quality Agenda

A great deal of the management thinking that surrounds the obsession with 'quality' stems from work that contributed to the rebuilding of Japan's industry base after the Second World War. An American academic and consulting engineer called William

Edwards Deming helped the Japanese to improve design, product quality, service and sales through various methods; not least the application of statistical methods. One of Edwards Deming's key philosophies was that time spent on improving the quality of a product or service actually reduced overall costs. It's interesting to notice how quickly this notion is forgotten in times of economic downturn.

Working independently of Edwards Deming, but arriving at a complementary idea, J.M. Juran (also teaching in Japan) urged organizations to focus on their longer-term outputs and outcomes. He argued that the maintenance of current processes and procedures was not enough (akin to treading water against the tide) and urged his clients to focus on longer term goals that required *continuous improvement*. Thus, he believed, the driver of true quality is change.

Following the revolution in Japanese industry, American industry faced a crisis in the 1970s and 1980s. Manufacturers were losing market share to Japanese products largely due to the superiority of quality of the Japanese products. In response to the situation, businessman and author Philip Crosby founded the principle of 'doing it right the first time' (or DIRFT). He also placed an emphasis on the place of people in an organization, and stressed that quality *encompassed all people, all systems and all the communications*.

In short 'total quality' is a continuous investment that reaches to all parts of an organization.

This agenda is explored comprehensively by the book *Total Quality: Success through People* (Collard, 2006), which provides an approach centred on the employees of an organization (as opposed to its systems and processes) and is thus helpful for the trainer or facilitator. Quality in an organization relies on consistency across the piece, each individual balancing their creativity and talents with consistent output.

Of course, many organizations have a structure in place to confirm their quality management processes in the form of the ISO9000 family of standards (ISO being an abbreviation of the International Organization of Standardization). Their specific requirements for this certification change over time, however, the type of general indicators of organization quality management may include:

- monitoring of all key processes to ensure effectiveness;
- keeping adequate records;
- regularly checking output (whether product or service) for defects;
- taking appropriate corrective action where necessary;
- regularly reviewing the quality process itself for effectiveness;
- facilitating continual improvement of systems and processes.

Yet it's one thing for an organization to be aligned to the principles of quality, to understand what its objectives are and have the right ethos, but another for it to be able to meet the requisite targets and goals with consistency. Consistency is a huge component of quality in both production and service, but consistency of action is not the same as consistency of thought, as the latter implies a lack of creativity. It's also in this case not about blindly repeating an action without understanding the need for that action (which we'll get to presently). In this context, consistency refers to achieving an agreed target of excellence repeatedly, no matter what. In such a form it's very simple to recreate in an experiential training setting.

It's not enough that we do our best, sometimes we have to do what is required.

Winston Churchill (Statesman)

We devised the following activity for a client who wanted a more consistent level of procedure from their teams, but wouldn't give us a great deal of time with them. We had to devise something that quickly allowed the group to develop a consistent process in which quality performance was rewarded, adequate performance was accepted but there were negative ramifications for an inadequate or catastrophic performance. We once also ran it as part of a school science lesson to get the students thinking about consistent weighing, measuring and recording when working in groups.

Exercise Idea – Target Performance

This is an exercise for two to eight learners. It can sit in a session as part of a discussion around consistent processes, or as part of a session around planning. It can also work as a session opener, although you may find it a little long for this purpose. It's also worth mentioning that you'll need to experiment a little before you run it, to determine what the acceptable parameters for the distances involved in the exercise are. We've provided suggestions, but these can and should be altered dependent on age and ability of the group and the carpet or table covering. You can also alter the number of balls in the stockpile, the respective scores of good and adequate performance, and the punishments appropriate to reflect the severity of inadequate performance in the learners 'real' world.

Time allowed: 25 minutes (includes briefing but not review).

Kit required: Approximately 30 marbles. You need a fixed quantity that allows each group member to have the same number of turns (that is, if you have six in a team they get five each, if you have four people they get eight each and so on).

Pieces of tubing (toilet or kitchen roll inners are fine). You need one per group.

Chalk or masking tape.

A stopwatch or clock.

This exercise also requires a long stretch of flat surface. A meeting room floor, conference table or corridor could all be suitable.

The set up: Chalk or tape out a target on the floor as shown in Figure 8.1 below. There should be a zone to represent excellent performance, adequate performance and inadequate performance. You may even wish to copy this diagram (and scoring system) on to a flipchart so that the learners have it for constant reference. Also mark out a 'launch line'(about four to five metres from the target) and a 'safety line' (about one metre further back).

Give the marbles and tube to the group. Permit no kit other than the tube and marbles, though you can use your own discretion as to how creative you allow teams to be in their problem-solving.

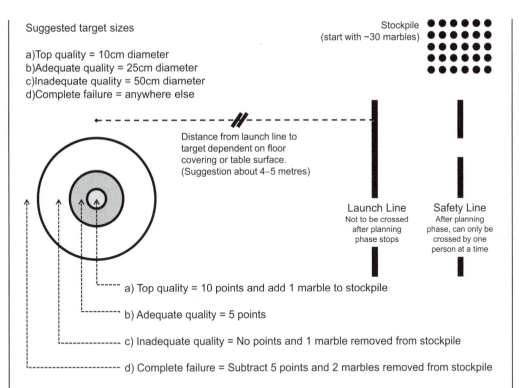

Suggested target sizes

a)Top quality = 10cm diameter
b)Adequate quality = 25cm diameter
c)Inadequate quality = 50cm diameter
d)Complete failure = anywhere else

Stockpile
(start with ~30 marbles)

Distance from launch line to
target dependent on floor
covering or table surface.
(Suggestion about 4–5 metres)

Launch Line
Not to be crossed
after planning
phase stops

Safety Line
After planning
phase, can only be
crossed by one
person at a time

a) Top quality = 10 points and add 1 marble to stockpile

b) Adequate quality = 5 points

c) Inadequate quality = No points and 1 marble removed from stockpile

d) Complete failure = Subtract 5 points and 2 marbles removed from stockpile

Figure 8.1   Equipment set-up for 'Target Performance' exercise

Explain to the group that this is an exercise designed to test their ability to plan and then implement a system of consistent quality. The objective of the exercise is to score as many points as possible in the time allowed. They score points by using the tube to roll marbles from the launch line on to the target.

A marble that stops in the 'top quality' zoned centre of the target will score ten points. In addition that marble will be added back into their stockpile of marbles.

A marble that stops in the 'adequate quality' zone will receive five points, and the marble will be removed from the game (by the trainer).

A marble that stops in the 'inadequate quality' zone will receive no points, and be removed from the game (by the trainer). However, as a result of this poor performance, one marble is removed from the team's stockpile.*

A marble that misses the target altogether ('complete failure') will result in a loss of five points, and two marbles being removed from the stockpile.

Explain that it is an exercise in two parts. You could even photocopy the following and hand it to the team.

Note: * Like a customer who has a poor experience tells another potential customer not to shop at that store, losing the store potential profit.

Part One – Planning Phase – ten minutes

The first part is the 'planning phase' and in that time you may move anywhere and devise, pilot and test a system to use the tube to launch marbles from the 'launch line' on to the target. Each member of the team must understand the chosen system and be able to implement it consistently. You have ten minutes to pilot, test, perfect and standardize your operation across the team. Scoring does not start until the 'implementation phase'.

Part Two – Implementation Phase – ten minutes

In the 'implementation phase' you must take it in turns to roll your marbles. Each team member must roll an equal number of marbles. Each team member may only roll *one* marble before handing the tube to another team member.

The tube and the person rolling the marble may not cross the launch line at any point. Breaking this rule will result in 'complete failure' and associated penalty, for that marble.

During the 'implementation phase' all team members not actually rolling the marble at any given time must stay behind the safety line. Breaking this rule will result in 'complete failure' and associated penalty, for that marble.

Individual scores will be called by the trainer, but it is the group's responsibility to keep tally of their total score.

Once all the marbles have been rolled, the exercise is complete and your score will be final.

After ten minutes the exercise will cease regardless of how many marbles are left in the stockpile.

During the exercise, remove the marbles from the target as soon as they've been rolled, and put them aside or back in the stockpile as dictated by performance. Ensure the timings are adhered to.

Target Performance: Additional Ideas

Use different-sized marbles in the initial stockpile, so groups have to plan multiple solutions to achieve consistent quality.

Reduce the time of the 'implementation phase' to increase the pressure on the group.

Suggest a target (about 150) and have the group beat it.

Make conditions or reward performance dependent (150 gets you pudding at lunch time…)

At the start of the planning phase blindfold one team member.

As with all the exercise suggestions and ideas presented here, this as an exercise is only as good as the enquiries which precede it and the learning review which follows it. Preceding questions might include:

In this team, what is quality performance?

How good is good enough?

How important is it that quality is consistent?

What are the ramifications if this standard is not met?

What checks and measures do you currently have in place to ensure quality is met?

How effective are these?

These questions would get the group thinking about quality performance, consistency of action and how replicable these notions are across the organization.

Once the activity has been completed you may want use these types of learning review questions:

What were the parallels between this and your day-to-day operations?

How did you decide on a strategy?

What value system does this reveal?

How was effective was your cross-team training process?

How did you ensure that your implementation was consistent?

Did you reach an adequate level of consistency?

Did things go to plan and how did you cope when they didn't?

What does this tell you about what needs to happen from today onwards back in the workplace?

Since quality is an attitude that influences all parts of an organization, and measuring quality is about benchmarking in some way against customer satisfaction or consistency of produce, then quality performance (whether production or service) can be easily explored experientially in a huge number of ways.

Again, before creating an exercise, it's helpful to start with a number of pre-design enquiries or conversations, such as:

Practitioner's Enquiries

What is 'quality' within the organization?

What would be good enough? What would be excellent? What would be better than excellent?

What would an improvement of quality mean to the people with whom you are working? (For instance, a reduction of the amount of rework, a cut in the number of complaints, or a pre-emptive measure such as better records and better dialogues with the team?)

To what extent could your internal people be treated as customers? Such a concept challenges the notion that in-house quality can be questionable if the exterior face is polished.

To what extent does everyone understand the systems that are in place and, more importantly, why those systems have been put in place in the first instance?

What are the barriers between departments?

Are actual facts and figures being recorded so that progress can benchmark and measured?

How do they *know* that their outputs are fit for purpose?*

Notice that these enquiries and conversations could equally act as pre-exercise primers to get a group engaged with the concepts of quality and the understanding of an organization.

Note: * This is easier to ratify in a product, but less so in a service. As a trainer, I spend a great deal of time with clients who use feedback forms for delegates on the day of the course. This doesn't, however, tell them anything about behavioural change in the workplace; it doesn't ask for triangulation of finding with, for example, a line manager of the course delegate; it gives them no longitudinal data; it simply tells the client that the delegate had a good (or bad) day away from the office. Is this measurement really fit for purpose? As a trainer or manager, if you want more information on this area, you may wish to read Donald Kirkpatrick's (Kirkpatrick, 1994) work on evaluating training.

Quality Exercise Idea One	Facilitator Notes and Thoughts
Give the group a simple task to do. This can be anything, from passing juggling balls to each other in certain orders to laying a table for a dinner party. Have them repeat the same task a number of different times with an improvement in quality each time. Ask them to decide on what quality might mean. Increase pressure by decreasing time, and requiring that they maintain the quality standard that they set.	Is quality always measurable? Certainly numerical markers of progress offer motivational possibilities and allow benchmarking, but are 'markers' quality or just a measure thereof? How do you truly measure the quality of a person's contribution? As a facilitator you may wish to question and challenge the vagaries within a group discussion. For instance, 'some', 'mostly', 'nearly' and 'try' aren't words that crop up too often in Quality Standards!

Quality Exercise Idea Two	Facilitator Notes and Thoughts
Present the group with a fictional (or real) organization and ask them to act as quality consultants. Sample organizations should be of a scale that is daunting on first impression, such as the NHS or the police service. Give them a set amount of time to creatively brainstorm how they would go about improving 'quality' in that organization.	Quality is often difficult to articulate as it reaches all parts of an organization, and is considered as an outcome as opposed to a hard, fast measurable output. By asking a group to investigate quality across an enormous organization, they must first understand what quality might mean in that context, and become specific and real in order to deal with it. This specific reality can then be copied back into their real-life workplaces.
Quality Exercise Idea Three	**Facilitator Notes and Thoughts**
Give the group plain paper, scissors, coloured pencils, rulers and glue. Require that they design, manufacture and produce differently coloured 5cm³ cubes to exact specifications to certain time limited targets. Provide each group with a list of customer demands, some of which should be highly specific (cubes should be exactly 5cm across, no area should remain uncoloured, no joins should protrude) and some should be ambiguous (the colourations should be decorative, the joins must be secure). As targets are met, increase the number of units demanded by the customer and decrease the time intervals.	As the customer, be contrary in cases of unexplored ambiguity ('*that's* not what I would call decorative colouring') and wise groups will ask for ambiguities to be clarified up front. Change your demands with each new batch order. Encourage the group to focus away from the task itself and on to a quality process by being ambiguous in the brief. Groups will impose their own quality definitions on the outputs of the task. The ambiguity allows them to be wrong, meaning they must continually change their quality control mechanisms and focus on customer satisfaction even as the pressure increases.
Quality Exercise Idea Four	**Facilitator Notes and Thoughts**
Have the group devise a prioritized list of 20–30 'customer quality indicators' which would indicate a good quality customer experience in a supermarket. Take them to a supermarket and ask them to act as secret shoppers to check whether their *own* quality indicators are being met. (This exercise would work well with any given workplace, but the customer element provides an easy conduit. If a supermarket is not easily accessible, then a staff canteen or nearby pub, restaurant or café would work as well. In the case of these substitutes this would also work as a lunch break activity.)	This type of field trip experience would pose an interesting experience for groups new to the notion of service and non-product quality. There is interesting territory in the differences between the group's list and the reality of the retail establishment, which has probably spent a great deal of time and money on improving the quality of customer service. Review around the parallels between that experience and what 'quality' is within their product or service. Prioritizing the list ensures that a group focuses on what is really important, and so what the key (Pareto's principle) areas of quality are.

There are many case studies available to purchase that raise awareness of quality processes within an organization; the one that we've used in the past is *Total Quality: An Awareness Building Exercise* (Lynch, 1991), which is excellent. However, all of the processes that these case studies use can be appropriated by the creative trainer. Here we present a few ideas (Quality Exercise Ideas, One to Five) that could easily be adapted to any type of organizational situation. We've also included some challenging enquiries that are equally useful to a trainer and learners alike.

Quality Exercise Idea Five	Facilitator Notes and Thoughts
In a large group environment, divide the group and have each sub-group make a packed lunch for each member of another group. Provide multi-choice lunch order forms at the start of the session and collect them in. Later in the session provide raw sandwich making materials, and distribute order forms to the groups. Have groups plan their quality strategy and then give them a very limited time to prepare each other's food. Distribute feedback forms to all, and have groups review each other's work around their quality management strategy versus their feedback.	You may want to check on your corporate health and safety policies if you decide to use this. The only times I've used exercises including food production have been with students who are generally less fussy and more expendable...The safety measure within it is the mutually assured quality marker that someone else in the exercise is making *your* lunch. This type of exercise (which I've adapted from a leadership exercise I saw many years ago) contains valuable material about quality, standards, customer feedback and execution of pre-planned production strategy against a tight deadline.

In spite of the value of a consistent execution of an action, quality comes from not only understanding the organization and its vision, but also from an understanding of the reason for that vision. To have real quality within an organization employees must understand not just the brains and hands of the beast, but its heart and soul as well.

Values, Missions and Quality

People who honestly mean to be true really contradict themselves much more rarely than those who try to be 'consistent'.

Oliver Wendell Holmes Jr. (Justice of US Supreme Court)

Drivers for quality come from the vision for the organization and the strategy and tactics by which we hope to arrive there. There is however more to it than that. Bo Burlingham, in the book *Small Giants* (2007), says that a 'vision is something that you plan to achieve, a mission is ongoing'.

Moreover, the writer Tom Peters[1] notes that great organizations originate from people who have 'not totally stupid obsessions' around which they build. Obsessions such as customer service, hospitality and attention to detail are the foundation stones around which quality and success is often based. Notice how these are things that are hard to measure. Yet if people understand, believe in and can behave in a way that is true to the organization's values and mission then they won't need operant conditioning to behave in a consistent way for the sake of it.

Allowing a group of learners to have simulated mission and values-based experiences can be easy to do. For instance, have them decide on which charity the company should support, in what way and to what extent (within certain boundaries). This immediately pushes a values-based decision on to a group. However, it is a little harder to easily and experientially square a values-based decision with the cold, hard face of commercial profit and loss. In order to do this we sometimes use this type of experiential exercise.

---

1   Co-author with Robert Waterman Jr. of the book *In Search of Excellence* (2004).

Exercise – The Top Quality Toy Company

Time required: About one hour (depending on numbers of groups). Not including review.

Number of participants: Groups of four to six.

Kit required: Household recyclable rubbish. Stationery cupboard essentials.

The set-up: Provide the participants with certain stationery cupboard essentials (glue, tape and so on) a box of empty and clean household rubbish (such as aluminium drinks cans, yoghurt pots, cereal packets, milk cartons and so on). These junk items represent metaphorical construction materials. We've presented three here as examples, but use and adapt depending on what you collect. Provide the groups with certain information about the materials (again, we've provided ideas below, but you might also use other factors such as shipping miles). The essential element is that groups are required to make decisions about the grade and durability of the material and the provenance of its source, against its cost. You may also wish set prices on tape and glue and so on.

Example Component	Option	Quality of Material	Material Details	Cost/ Unit
Juice carton	A	High grade Long-lasting	Low sustainability. Amazonian mahogany.	£5
	B	Medium grade	High sustainability. Responsibly sourced from constantly replaced Scandinavian pine.	£4
	C	Low grade and dubious quality	High sustainability. Produced from recycled landfill.	£1
Plastic cup	A	High grade	Produced with new environmentally-friendly green plastic moulding technology.	£10
	B	Medium grade	Produced using traditional methods – less environmentally sound.	£5
	C	Medium grade	Produced in third-world sweatshop.	£1
Kitchen roll inner	A	Low grade Dubious quality	Sourced from recycled Christmas trees.	£4
	B	High grade	Sourced from Slash'n'Burn Logging company. Questionable provenance.	£2
	C	Medium grade	Sourced by Fairworld Trading Co. from a responsible source.	£10

The Exercise

Give each group a certain amount of time (about 45 minutes) to design and build a new and original prototype child's toy from the components.

In this time they should also develop and decide on:

1) A rigorous testing policy to ensure quality manufacturing for their toy.

2) An advertisement and marketing campaign for launching the toy into a competitive marketplace (if you're feeling creative you could provide facts and figures about what pricing the marketplace will take in certain sectors).

3) A price for the finished item (showing profit margins per unit).

4) A statement regarding their sustainability and ethical policies.

At the end of the allotted time have them present their work, finances and ethical statement to the rest of the room, who must ask them challenging questions about their product, cost and values decisions.

This exercise offers more potential discussion scope than other build-type exercises because of the toy element, which means groups tend to make much more values-driven decisions. They need to ask, 'What *sort* of company do we want to be?' It also allows groups to trade-off certain types of values (for instance, ethical material sourcing) for others (grade of build material or cost). In addition, by requiring a marketing and sales campaign, it also encourages groups to think about who their *customer* is. Is it the parent with the money or the child? They need to engage with what *type* of customer concerns they are most interested in, since the concerns of a child ('Is this toy fun to play with?') may be different from that of their parents ('Is this item educational/safe?' or 'Will it keep them quiet for long?' or 'Will this require hundreds of batteries?' and so on). Also, the requirement of building a toy means that customer safety and vigorous testing of build quality should be paramount, and of course every team member will understand in a multitude of ways what a quality toy could and must be.

As usual, the benefit to learning from this type of exercise comes from the post-task review. Rather than the teamwork-type of questions (such as: 'Who led and followed and why?', 'How did you divide the workload?' and so on), you may wish to focus on quality, values and mission. For example, typical questions about the exercise may include:

The Top Quality Toy Company – Review Questions

How did you decide on a strategy? What factors affected your decisions?

Which factors and decisions carried the greatest weight?

What was most important to your group?

Did you all agree what was important and how soon did you reach that decision?

What came first, the values or the toy idea? (Notice how the process you asked them to go through echoes the process outlined in the opening chapter of this book, about creative exercise design.)

To what extent were your values obvious to the consumer through the marketing and sales approaches that you adopted?

To what extent did your values decision affect the quality of product and associated services?

Do 'values' come at a premium price?

How did you manage the inherent conflicts that values-based decisions can bring in a commercial or competitive environment?

You may then wish to continue the learning discussions with questions that focus the agenda back on to the real world, such as:

What are the values that this (that is, the real) organization/team holds to be important?

How do you know? (Is there agreement across the groups?)

What is this organization's/team's mission? (Mission statement?)

To what extent do you buy into this? To what extent did it affect your decision to work here?

To what extent are these obvious to the outside world?

How do the values and mission affect the quality of product/service that you offer?

If you could select new values and mission, what would they be? How would these be made real in the workplace?

As mentioned in the introduction to the book, I've sat in mission meetings before, and I must admit that I never really understood why we were having them. I'd never understood (until I became an outside agent with responsibility for my own organization) how much these nebulous and unquantifiable concepts shaped every part of what we do. I'd certainly never really had to consciously set a course by them or define a strategy based upon them. Learning experiences such as this one described can provide at least some insight into this type of thinking, and open up huge new areas for discussion.

The previous exercises raise a number of issues in a group such as the way that a strategy is disseminated, shared and standardized across a diverse group of people. Even in a company or organization that is well aligned, the sharing of information can prove a real stumbling block. This difficulty is usually amplified as the organization grows in size. Add in political in-fighting and jostling for resource within the different arms of the organization and the ownership and exchange of information becomes a real concern indeed. Elsewhere in this book we talk about how a creative trainer can help facilitate discussions *within* teams – yet many of the problems that surround 'information' concerns those exchanges that are *between* teams.

Where is all the knowledge we lost with information?

T.S. Eliot (Poet)

Information Transfer within Organizations

In the book *Analysing Organizations*, Sandra Dawson (1989) identifies the following problems with the passage of information from one part of an organization to another:

- *Differing Value*: Quantifiable information takes precedence over non-quantifiable information in decision-making.
- *Verification and Validation*: How close to truth is the information and can the information be validated by a third party?
- *Neutrality*: Information is rarely used in a wholly objective way.
- *Scarcity*: 'Good' information is scarce and expensive.
- *Hierarchies*: Even within informal networks some information carries more weight than other.
- *Gatekeepers*: These control information behind physical, social or technical barriers.
- *Partiality*: Information cannot be completely transmitted, and what information is transferred can be reflective of an individual's own interests.
- *Suppression*: Some information can be withheld or excluded (deliberately or unconsciously) if it counters the dominant view.

On top of a consistent execution of a values and mission driven performance, if a real and 'total' improvement of quality is to be reached and maintained, then (to return to Philip Crosby's 'Do It Right First Time' edict from earlier in the chapter) it must encompass all people, all systems and *all the communications*.

So how, as a creative facilitator, can you create experiences designed to experientially simulate the flow of information from one part of an organization to another, and more importantly illustrate the *benefit* of doing so?

As usual the set-up and preceding enquiries set your tone for whatever the specific learning is that you want to extract from the process. Questions such as these may be useful:

Practitioner's Enquiries

What type of information do you value most highly?

What restricts the flow of information from one part of a process to another?

How processed is the information before it is shared?*

From which sources is information more valued?

What would be the actual benefit of improved informational flow?

Note: In my previous professional career as a research scientist, most information was highly processed before it was shared, and only the 'best' information was published. 'Best' in this context does not necessarily indicate a judgement of quality.

Informational flow can be restricted in an experiential learning set-up by altering the rules regarding intake and sharing of information. For instance, asking the group to carry out a task blindfolded or forbidding them from talking affects the informational flow. While such exercises can be hugely useful, sometimes it is necessary to increase the realism a little to help groups to understand the point you wish to make.

To give an example of how informational flow can be manipulated in a semi-real setting we've provided an exercise here. This type of exercise is ideal for a project team who are coming together for the first time. It can also be used to illustrate collaborative working or cross-departmental conflict and processes. You should note that this is an exercise idea, and a semi-formed recipe for delivering it. It works (we've used it on a number of occasions) but in the interests of space we've not included the full participant briefs here for you. The idea of *process* is the valuable and transferable element, and we've provided the process in full. Be creative and flesh the details out for yourself to suit your geography and your organization.

Exercise Idea – Departmental Secondments

The objective of the exercise is for a group of disparate departments within a simulated manufacturing organization to come together to work out the ideal site for a new factory. This could equally be a school, hospital, university or business park, though the details would need changing.

Time required: At least 75 minutes.

Number of participants: A minimum of six (but the exercise works best with between 12 and 24 people).

Kit required: Plenty of different coloured stickers and at least one large scale* map of any area, the more the better but multiple maps must be identical. It helps if it shows diverse terrain (some urban areas, some countryside) and it should show major roads, rail links airports and so on. A few pages from a glove-box road atlas appropriately stuck together would serve well, but an Ordnance Survey-type map is better.

Create a number of contrasting briefs (at least six). These should reflect the interests of different parts of the organization and should have some back-story, consistent between briefs – general information about the company. They should also have some specific information reserved for each 'department'. Each brief should be two to three sides in length, and most of it should be similar, only the specific departmental facts and figures (about one to two sides) should differ. In addition, you might want to alter the *quality* of the information. Some could be hard and fast numerical data and some could be more qualitative. Some should be non-negotiable for that department, and some should be desirable considerations but not essential.

However, what should be consistent between the groups is the instruction that, using only their own departmental agenda, they should work out the perfect location for the company's new plant.

To give an idea of the types of department we use, here are six reasonable generic ones in shortened form. These would of course be far more fleshed-out in reality.

Human Resources	The new factory will generate hundreds of new jobs and so HR is interested in proximity to a source of potential employees. Tax breaks for training and developing people in more deprived areas. Public transport (bus routes and rail access) of vital importance.
Shipping	Interested in proximity to road and rail links. Nearness to ports (sea or air) also important. Good motorway links required. Near other commerce would be advantageous.
External Relations	Difficulties of maintaining company's 'sustainable' image if building new site on greenbelt land. Kudos and PR advantages of creating new jobs near city X.
Infrastructure	Need for utilities such as gas, electricity and water. Lower utilities rates in area Y. Need for district to create new link roads and so on.
Finance and Land Purchase	Land use in inner city, very expensive and becomes progressively cheaper away from certain urban areas. Tax breaks for building in certain areas.
Architecture and Build Costs	Building costs increase as site moves further from urban areas. Architecture becomes more expensive as site moves into heritage region.

If you only have one map, lay it out in the centre of the room, and ask all of the participants to come and study it for a couple of minutes. While they are perusing the locale, distribute the briefs (and duplicate maps if you have them) into different areas of the room to create the departments. Then separate out the group equally into these six departments. If you have six people, one person represents a whole department. If you have 12, 18, or 24 the department has two, three or four people. Uneven group sizes do not affect the exercise.

Give the groups ten minutes to read the brief individually and a further ten to discuss it within their department and then come and restudy the map, but do not allow intra-departmental discussion.

After 15 minutes go round the groups (individually) and ask them to provide a grid reference for their proposed site. You may wish to write a two-line instruction into the brief about how to provide grid references appropriate to the map you use. Record these carefully. If you can locate another identical map, it is worth having a copy that is only to be viewed by you. Use coloured stickers or to mark their recommendations on your map, but leave the master map blank.

After the groups have provided an initial solution, ask the participants to leave their paperwork at the departmental base and then redistribute the group. In essence, what you must do here is leave some of the department at home and send others out on secondment to other groups.**

Give all of the groups ten minutes of fact-finding discussion (or solo reading if low participant numbers), with the instruction being that the person who has remained at their 'home' department should brief the visitor fully about that department's needs and drivers.

Ask everyone to return to their home group and give them a further ten minutes of discussion and reporting back. With the new information in their possession, and combined with their original data, now ask each department to provide you with a revised grid reference for their proposal for the factory site. Again, this information should be collected by you only and not shared with the room as a whole. Ensure you record these data in a way that differentiates them from those collected before this first secondment. For example: red dots for round one, blue dots for round two.

Then repeat the secondment process ensuring that a) those who stayed behind before get a to visit another department and b) there aren't repeat visits to the same department (so if a representative of 'shipping' went to 'HR' in round one, another 'shipping' member shouldn't visit 'HR' again). Again, give all of the groups ten minutes of fact-finding discussion, and then have them return to base.

Finally, give each home department ten minutes to discuss their new data and decide upon their best choice for a final site for the factory. In this time ask them to prepare a *one-minute* presentation to the Board of which site they would choose, and what key rationale they used to make their decision. A nice touch here is to stick the master map on the wall and allow them during the presentation to mark their final choices with (for example, yellow) stickers for all to see.

At this point you may wish to chair a final open discussion about the final site placement, but in our experience this is not usually required to make the point of the exercise.

After the exercise has concluded explain the colouring of the stickers on the map. Ask the groups to reflect upon how their original positions changed with new information from their fact-finding secondments. Draw whatever conclusions are required from the placement of dots on the map. Sometimes the dots converge towards a consensus answer, and sometimes they appear random. Some groups' positions change wildly from round to round, sometimes they remain resolute. *The beauty of the stickered grid reference is that it illustrates very simply how new information changes perspectives and positions across the organization as a whole.*

Additional Exercise Idea

Create a separate 'executive group' who must make the ultimate decision on the site location and who have agendas of their own. These agendas can be based on the company's best interest or purely selfish (for example, they don't want to commute more than 15 miles). Keep the executive group removed from the secondment process, but allow them to fact-find at any point with any group and let them chair the final meeting. After the final meeting give the rest of the group a five-minute break and ask the executive group make a final decision to present to the group.

Note: * Suggested scale: 1:250,000 is about right, where 4cm on the map is equal to 10km; ** If you only have six people, move everyone one department clockwise. If you have six to twelve people, move half of each department one place clockwise and leave the other at base. If you have more than twelve, leave one member at base and move some of the rest of the team one place and some two. This sounds complicated, but in reality isn't.

The central notion of illustrating how information affects decisions within organizations using very simple dots on a map is however replicable, without many of the facts and figures that surround it in this case, in far simpler forms; but compared to the other exercises and ideas presented in this book, 'secondment' is quite a long one. As such it needs a lengthy and deep review in order to extract the maximum amount of value.

How to Review this Exercise

The types of questions that you may want to have groups discuss after the conclusion of the exercise are:

What were the benefits to the organization as a whole of cross-departmental information flow? How do these translate to your own organization?

What are the benefits of greater cross-departmental knowledge to any *individual* within the organization?

At what point does this sort of information sharing become unwieldy and impractical? How much does any given individual *need* to know about the workings of a different part of the organization?

To avoid this impractical attempt at cross-workforce omniscience, usually organizations have mid-management precisely so that key individuals from separate departments can talk with their counterpart in another. What are the pros and cons of such hierarchic arrangements?

What types of information and argument carried more weight? Qualitative or quantitative? Hard or soft? Why? (An interesting corollary here is the notion of whether quality is always measurable.)

What information did you decide to share and what did you reserve?

How much credibility did you give to another group's data and position?

How objective and apolitical were you when briefing your secondment visitor?

Did you view the information from some sources as being more worthwhile than that from others?

How protective of 'your' departmental agenda did you become? What were the consequences of this?

To understand the nature of the people one must be a prince, and to understand the nature of the prince, one must be of the people.

Niccolo Machiavelli (Political Philosopher)

Understanding the way that an organization operates completely is clearly an immense task, and yet some insight, combined with an appreciation of quality processing and effective informational flow can offer *any* employee huge returns, from the top of the organization to the base. Moreover, *integration* of these facets is invaluable and in this regard creative training experiences can be used to real purpose. If different parts of the organization understand each other better then rivalries and infighting may start to diminish, and creativity can start to flourish; if the context for an organization flows from a clear source at the top and the ideas have a channel to flow upwards, and if the means of communication is chosen to best suit the people and the message, then companies and organizations can do great things.

In order to do all this, people need to talk to each other. Helping them to do this more effectively is the subject of the next chapter.

CHAPTER 9

Getting People Talking: Building Productive Relationships

A good quartet is like a good conversation among friends interacting to each other's ideas.

Stan Getz (Jazz Musician)

In Chapter 3, we examined the Johari Window as a model that can be used to illustrate the advantage to the individual's development of working with others. It is often the case that I will learn and develop through the relationship I have with others, but this can only ever be true if there is communication between us. As I share my experience and insights with others, and they share theirs with me, each of us will grow and develop in ways which would be very elusive if not impossible if left to ourselves.

Of course, the kind of communication that we need in order to enrich our learning is not the trite, mundane conversation of day-to-day 'small talk'. I did not learn anything meaningful when I had a conversation with the woman in the corner shop this morning about how we both forget how much we like peanut butter. I don't share anything of myself when an acquaintance asks how I am and I tell them that I am 'fine'.

Learning conversations are riskier, richer, deeper and ultimately more insightful than the conversation we usually share with casual acquaintance. This chapter aims to examine some of the aspects of learning conversations and explore some ways of encouraging people to talk in this way.

One of the joys of facilitation for me is the privilege of being able to watch as people learn from each other. They might take notes or look studiously at a hand-out when I introduce them to a piece of theory or give them some information, but it is when they listen to *each other*, or when they find themselves being listened to and affirmed when they share an insight, that the *real learning* often takes place. It could be that my place as a facilitator is to speed up the process of learning through communication, or it could be that there is a problem that requires remedial attention. Either way, the place of a facilitator in this situation is to be a catalyst for others' communication and consequent learning.

The most influential of all educational factors is the conversation in a child's home.

William Temple (Logician)

People learn from the conversations they have, as children learn from what surrounds them in the home. If participants are provided with a fatuous conversation filled with truisms and clichés in the training room, they will learn that training is of limited use in their daily lives. The trick for a skilled facilitator is to ensure that they are provided with positive, rich conversational material from which to draw their own conclusions.

However self-sufficient the people in your sessions are, it is worth remembering that in a 'real' learning environment, by nature of the learning process, most people will be vulnerable. There is often a little posturing from those who feel they 'should' be confident, some withdrawal by those who are naturally a little reticent and recourse to cliché and previously learned facts from those who are keen to supply answers quickly. For real conversation to take place, it is necessary that those participating feel confident in their surroundings to be themselves and to risk exposing their vulnerability at whatever level is appropriate for the learning to be genuine.

As a facilitator, your role is to encourage an environment where this confidence is protected, encouraged and nurtured. This will start at the very outset of your session.

Ice-Breakers: Not Just a 'Bit of Fun'

'Ice-breakers' are often the subject of derision (particularly if called such). However, having some kind of activity at the start of your session which encourages people to talk will clear the way for increased depth of conversation later.

My experience is that people are more likely to wade into a learning conversation if they have paddled in the shallows of an easy conversation earlier. The shallowness of the initial conversation will depend a little on how much time you have to spare. If time is limited, it may be wise to introduce the topic of your session at this stage;

Practitioner's Exercise

Consider the theme of any possible training session.

Write down seven simple questions (ones which need no context or explanation) which would encourage people to start thinking about the session theme and talk to each other at a deeper level than a basic welcoming introduction might do.

Such questions might be:

What is 'effectiveness' and is it different to 'efficiency'?

Who is the best communicator you know, and upon what evidence do you base your judgement?

How would you manage *you* if you were your boss?

Note that these questions are thought-provoking but safe and require evidences and answers that will act as seeds for potential discussions later.

---

perhaps by placing a number of questions on individual strips of paper, designed to get people thinking and talking about the subject at hand. I have often found it useful to project a 'welcome' instruction for when participants enter the room, telling them to make themselves comfortable, think and talk about a given theme.

What happens in the opening minutes of a session will not only set the tone for the rest of the intervention but it also, implicitly and explicitly, provides the learners with the rules of engagement for what is to follow.

> *In football, like in life, you must learn to play within the rules of the game.*
>   Hayden Fry (American Football Coach)

People value boundaries. Even if they enjoy pushing at them, most people like the boundary to be there and will feel uncomfortable if unsure of the expectations placed upon them. I usually (unless the learning point demands that I do otherwise) provide boundaries when I introduce a session, informing people of the finish time and any breaks, letting people know that I won't be providing all the answers, and so on.

When it comes to a group who will need to work together and discuss at a deeper level, I will sometimes ask them to set and agree the boundaries themselves. I rarely use the term 'ground rules' as just like 'ice-breaker' the term has negative connotations for some which can disrupt the positive impact of the concept. But in essence this is what I'm doing. Simply asking the group to discuss what is necessary for them to feel comfortable in group discussions can provide useful boundaries and frameworks for the participants to work within. Do take notes from this discussion and display the resulting framework throughout the session, especially if that agreement has been tested or violated.

Practitioner's Questions

When would it be appropriate to establish 'ground rules'? When would it not be useful?

How best could you elicit these *honestly* from a group? (See Part II concerned with 'Getting at the Honesty' page 35.)

What are *your* absolutely fundamental ground rules for group work?

How would you ensure that these were integrated with the group's own? Should you be covert or overt?

So it is that by sharing with others, an individual can enhance their own learning and their own learning environment. But of course, all the honest talking in the world is only useful to the speaker unless others are listening, *really* listening. Communication, by definition, must be two-way – both transmitted and received – for it truly to have taken place.

Getting People Listening

Most conversations are simply monologues delivered in the presence of witnesses.

Margaret Miller (Author)

For all people some of the time and for some people all of the time, 'listening' simply means, 'Ooh, I can't talk at the moment because someone else is speaking so I'll use this time to work out what I will say next.' This is very common (notice how often you do it yourself when in casual conversation) but is rarely helpful for anything beyond the maintenance of common courtesy.

Don't be tempted to make assumptions about whether people are really listening to one another or not. A friend of ours took on an apprentice, Jack, who fidgeted habitually and who seemed to be paying little attention. She was shocked, albeit pleasantly so, when, some weeks later, she noticed that Jack was, unprompted, applying intricate details from that previous instruction. Often the signals that we give can be horribly misleading.

Practitioner's Enquiries

What signals do you look for to indicate that someone is really, actively listening to you?

How do you ensure that you stay focused on the person or people to whom you are listening and not get distracted by your own agenda?

Do you pay more attention to their words or their tonality, or do you listen for a larger sense of what is really being said?

How could you encourage a group to listen more effectively and when would doing this be appropriate?

---

*To **listen** well, is as powerful a means of influence as to talk well, and is as essential to all true conversation.*

Chinese Proverb

Listening Exercises

We could have written a whole book on tricks and techniques for getting people to listen properly to each other. However, here are five quick exercises that will get people focused on what others say:

Aural Kim's Game Traditionally, Kim's game is a memory test of visual information. The name is derived from the Kipling's novel 'Kim' and the game comprises of a number of objects placed on a tray, one of which is then removed and must be identified.	Read out a list of 30 words. Wait for 30 seconds, randomize the order of the list and remove one of the words. Reread the now randomized and shortened list and ask the group to identify the missing word.
Autobiography and Test Questions	Group participants into pairs. Give one partner (the talker) a list of details they must cover as they tell (in three minutes) the story of their life so far. These details could be the name of their school, first pet, parents' occupations, first memory, best holiday and so on. When finished, issue some edict from the front, for example, 'There's been a slight change of plan, the break will now be at 11.20.' Just to take the focus away from the exercise. Partner B (the 'listener') must then answer five questions about Partner A's life story.
Potholing	In trios, have a group discuss an issue (the best topics or issues are the ones relevant to the issue at hand for the rest of the session). Give the instruction that, as one person is talking, the other two have to internally pretend that they are in a cave and hear everything in their head with just a *slight* echo. So they should internally repeat to themselves what their colleagues have just said. To do this successfully, mental processes need to be completely engaged with what another person is saying and so, in all probability, trains of thought will align.
I *Knew* You'd Say That	Have partners talk for two or three minutes on any given topic. Instruct partners to listen to the tone, content and sentiment in their colleague's message and to *mentally* finish their sentences for them. After the time has expired, have pairs exchange how accurate they were, and what led to increased or decreased accuracy.
Scrabble Challenge	Have participants draw a scrabble tile from a bag (first having removed x,z,q, and so on) They must then internally count the number of words that the group uses that start with a certain letter, during a five-minute discussion of any given issue. *Note, this can easily result in listening for details, but not necessarily paying attention to the content of what is being said. Either way it requires focus, and can promote interesting conversations about how hard a task it was.*

Conversation in Order to Further a Task

Yet, in true communication, more than simple listening is required. If a conversation is to progress productively, each contribution will have a *purpose*, will build on the previous one and will inform the big-picture of a group's working.

A while ago, I was facilitating a team of professionals who worked remotely from each other on a project that was additional to each of their day-jobs. They were meeting to look ahead and see what the future of their joint project might hold. I could see that they were each working to capacity on their full-time jobs and so time to dedicate to the project was a scarce commodity. This issue (and the fact that no one was talking about it) seemed to me to be the obstacle that was impeding their progress.

In order to test my notion, I made my assumption explicit that they all wanted to continue in their day-jobs rather than aspire to work full or even part time for the project. 'Yes,' stated the project leader assertively. 'That's right,' agreed one of the others. Then a third team member spoke up. 'Well,' he began uncertainly, 'six months ago I would have agreed with you. But things have changed a bit in my job and I've been just wondering…'

What followed was an animated discussion that would never have occurred had this large and vital, shared assumption not been stated openly. A whole range of possibilities opened up and although no one was able to commit to positive action at that point, the information that one of the key players *may* have been able to invest greater energy into the project changed the parameters of the task significantly and allowed for dramatically increased progress. As the session ended, the project leader commented that he had been reminded not to take the status quo for granted.

This is a great example of how, by discussion and communication, the benefits of working collaboratively are fully exploited and the whole truly becomes greater than the sum of the parts. If these people had been purely focused on the task at hand, it may have been sufficient for them all to continue as they were doing, not really communicating about their own wider priorities or their place in the future of the project and thus they simply work alongside each other, rather than capitalizing on working together.

> *The problem with communication…is the illusion that it has been accomplished.*
> George Bernard Shaw (Author)

If groups are to behave optimally, then they need complete (or as near as possible) information in order to gain *proper* perspective on the task at hand. This completeness includes insight that individuals possess on task, team processes and individual contributions and behaviour. As a facilitator, if you notice progress on a task beginning to stall, listen for a moment to the information that is being shared. Are the team working under a false, or at least a questionable assumption? Does someone have information that they are not sharing, or have not been given the opportunity to share? How might you facilitate greater communication amongst the group at this point, without imposing your opinion or detracting from the learning that is taken place?

We were working a couple of years ago with a rather dysfunctional project team. Some of the team were removed from the main part of the project and were meeting the project leader and the rest of the team by video-conference. We were working with the 'remote' group and were sitting in on one of those meetings. Towards the end of the meeting, one of the team members in our remote location put forward a radical solution to a problem that the project had been facing.

> *'Yes,'* said the boss (via the video link) *'that's **exactly** the sort of thing we should try to do.'*

Sitting as impartial observers in the room we could feel the remote team become energized at this decisive and bold management decision, and after the meeting had concluded they started to busy themselves on a strategy to implement the shared vision.

We, however, were not so inspired and suggested that they make a quick call to the boss to double check that this was what he had actually requested. 'Of course it is!' they said, 'What makes you think anything else?'

'Because, *exactly the sort* is a contradiction, *should* is possibly hypothetical and *try* is not the same as *do*.'

A short phone call confirmed our suspicions. The boss was talking hypothetically and hadn't really wanted that particular solution implemented. This lack of clear communication between team members, more than any other reason, was why the team were so dysfunctional.

This example seems almost farcical (and later, we were amused to see a similar conversation play out in a television satire) yet teams often communicate in strange ways, and sometimes it takes an impartial observer (or a new team member) to realize how ineffective the established means of dialogue can be.

Time to Reflect

Let's rest for a while, till our souls catch us up.
                    Bring On The Wonder (Susan Enan, Singer and Songwriter)

Of course, it may be that in the often fast pace of an activity-based day, it is difficult for people to articulate what they feel, or what they are learning. Some people, particularly those with a reflective style (see Section One), will need time to think and reflect individually before being able to effectively express themselves. This may not need to be a great deal of time, but do be aware (particularly if your own preference is less reflective) that a lack of meaningful response may not mean that a participant is not engaged or is 'shy'. I often find that a short break after a particularly challenging activity before asking the participants to review what they have learned pays large dividends. It can also be useful for all parties to get some fresh air. Encourage the participants to go for a brisk walk and come back ready to say the things that will get the group moving forward. Don't allow them to sit until they've said their piece – this will help to maintain energy and sharpen the focus of the conversation.

If the constraints of your training session permit, it can be useful to provide delayed ways to capture meaning, sometimes hours or days after the intervention. As a full-time in-house trainer I used to ensure that I held short debrief meetings a week or more after developmental events. The event participants involved found that it was useful to be able to distil what they had learned for a while after the adrenalin of the event had dissipated. To hold a conversation too soon after an event means that the topic of discussion might just be merely initial gut reactions to the success or otherwise of any venture.

Practitioner's Questions

For your interventions, what would be the optimal elapsed time between activity and learning discussion?

How might you artificially propagate learning if you don't have this amount of time?

What could you do to stop 'business as usual' invading the time between your intervention and the review conversation?

Drawing Out the Shy One

Confidence contributes more to conversation than wit.
Francois de La Rochefoucauld (Author)

Very early in my training and development career, I was working on a residential programme and I met Emma. Emma was a graduate student at a prestigious research institute and one of the most intelligent people that I had ever met. She had thought carefully about her own learning objectives for the programme; and these were not to practice teamwork, networking, project management or interpersonal effectiveness skills. Instead, her single success criterion was being able physically to stay in a group environment for the four days of the course.

Emma was shy to the point of debilitation. Not only was she reticent about sharing her ideas and reluctant to engage in social discourse with those around her, she was almost totally deficient in confidence both personally and professionally. Almost totally. In the middle of the course there was an artificial learning activity which required the group quickly to get to grips with a large amount of technical information, which happened to be in Emma's area of expertise. One of the other group members realized this and very quietly passed one of the copies of the information to Emma and said simply, 'We need your help with this.'

The transformation was amongst the most beautiful sights I have ever witnessed. Emma took the paper, scanned it silently and then began to quietly explain to the person who had asked her for help, what it meant. The group fell silent, focusing on the explanation she was providing, and then all deferred to her as she started to outline the implications for the activity.

I would love to write that this marked the end of Emma's diffidence and that she is now a leader in her field, confidently managing her own research group and speaking at international conferences, but I don't know. What I do know is that from that moment she started to grow and develop her confidence and contributions during the course. *I have never forgotten the powerful impact of simply noticing someone's skills and honestly asking for their help.*

People need to be confident in order to share in a conversation. If you as a facilitator notice that someone seems to be lacking in self-confidence, the answer is not to put them on the spot and insist that they share as much as their more apparently assured colleagues. Rather it is firstly to notice your assumptions and only then to meet them where they are and take them step by step into a place where their insights can benefit both themselves and the rest of the group.

Practitioner's Enquiries

Do you have a balance of types of activity across your designs, to maximize the chance of any individual being able to offer their expertise and contribute from a more secure space?

Before any activity, how might you encourage a group to build a more complete knowledge of all of the skills and abilities in the room?

During an activity, how might you as a facilitator encourage a group to use all of the talent available to them, especially if there is an imbalance of contribution?

Asking Questions

Questions provide the key to unlocking our unlimited potential.
Anthony Robbins (Coach and Writer)

At some point in our development as adults we stop asking questions constantly. We hold back, possibly out of 'politeness' or possibly for fear of being thought foolish if the answer to our question is perceived by others to be obvious. But if we as facilitators of learning are to encourage people to work with what is real rather than what is assumed, whether that is in the here and now or the bigger picture, we must encourage and model the asking of questions.

No question is so difficult to answer as that to which the answer is obvious.
Karl Otto von Schonhausen Bismarck (German Statesman)

If we ask questions in the course of our training and development interventions, let's make them good ones. In the opening chapter, we discuss the asking of different types of questions. There is no objectively established 'best' type of question, beyond the right enquiry in a given situation.

As an academic linguist, part of my role was to collect data by interviewing people and recording the conversations. We didn't mind *what* people said, as it was *how* they said it that was of primary interest to us. However, research has shown[1] that the best and most natural data was obtainable from people who were talking about subjects which engaged them, so I quickly learned the kinds of questions to ask that would (usually!) result in a person talking at length about something which they found interesting.

It may seem surprising, bearing in mind the cultural stereotype that the British are reserved, private folk who would rather discuss the weather than anything remotely personal, the best way to access the rich data I needed was to ask people about *themselves*, their memories of childhood, their experiences of fear (in some cases, even of mortal fear) and their families. A simple, 'What was it like around here when you were growing up?' or 'I bet that could be scary sometimes, couldn't it?' could sometimes unlock a monologue which could, given sufficient encouragement, extend for the full hour I needed.

---

1   If you're interested have a look at Chambers (1995) and Labov (1972).

It is rarely appropriate in a learning environment to ask questions about people's personal histories. However, the lesson I learned that I use in training settings was two-fold: most people are happier to share themselves than you might expect; and a small prompt can take you a long way.

Practitioner's Exercise

When was the last time you got someone to talk to you and really tell you how they felt about something, or what they learned in a given situation?

When you're in an appropriate social setting, take an opportunity to try out asking questions; then prompting your guinea pig to explore a little deeper.

Afterwards reflect on how the conversation went. Was it comfortable for you? For them? What happened? What could you do differently another time?

When People Fall Out

If you can just learn a simple trick, Scout, you'll get along a lot better with all kinds of folks. You never really understand a person until you consider things from his point of view...Until you climb inside of his skin and walk around in it.

From *To Kill a Mockingbird* by Harper Lee

Sometimes people disagree and it may become more than a simple difference of opinion. As soon as tempers start to flare, both communication and learning stops, so, Tuckman's 'storming' phase aside (see Chapter 3), raised voices and hurt feelings are not what you're aiming for in a training session.

However, as a facilitator, it can often be within your remit to help participants find the learning that can often emerge from disagreements, if possible without the sulking and the shouting.

In their book *Crucial Conversations*, Patterson et al. (2002) propose an elegant but straightforward model to use in these circumstances and, if employed by participants in the heat of the moment, this can help to regain a level of communication and assist in sharing information amongst a group.

S	Share your facts
T	Tell your story
A	Ask for others' experience
T	Talk tentatively
E	Encourage testing

The model works on the premise that when communication becomes difficult, this is the time to take nothing for granted. In a similar way to the Ladder of Inference (see Chapter 7, p. 114) this framework encourages people to start with what is *known* – the pool of information, not coloured by perspective or interpretation – to *'share the facts'*. If we start with expressing what is known, what is least controversial and least insulting, we can move on in the conversation, confident that we are building on a solid foundation.

Only after sharing the incontrovertible facts is it appropriate to *'tell your story'*. The facts alone do not give the full picture, as your reactions and feelings around the issue are relevant. However, it is important to 'own' these, making certain not to accuse. Statements starting 'I feel…' are less controversial than 'You make me…' and therefore allow information to be shared and the relevant points to be discussed.

When you have shared your facts and told your story, remember that by definition, dialogue needs two participants. *'Ask for others' experience'* – invite the other party or parties in the discussion to do what you have done, to share their route to the current position. Which facts are relevant for them, what is their story?

Be kind, for everyone you meet is fighting a hard battle.

Plato (Philosopher)

Stating the facts, telling a story and asking for others experiences will provide people with sufficient space and dignity to make an agreement that they are both/all genuinely happy with, provided that the steps are carried out according to the overarching instructions: *'talk tentatively'* and *'encourage testing'*. Talking tentatively refers to the basic skill of treating facts as facts, but stories (interpretations of or reactions to those facts) as stories. Prefacing a story statement with phrases such as 'I was wondering…' or 'I was feeling…' make the status of these contributions clear. Encouraging testing is a reminder to ask questions such as, 'Is that right?' or 'Is that how you see it?' and so on throughout the conversation.

Taking Conversations Deeper

This process can also work well for a learning facilitator. As professionals, we generally don't present ourselves as 'experts' who have all the answers, and neither do any of the people whose style we admire. This deliberately naïve approach to groups' issues can occasionally leave a facilitator feeling a little vulnerable. Recently, I was working with a group of people all of whom were considerably older than I and many of whom had known me for a long time. As such I was rather nervous. The issues they had asked me to facilitate discussion around were sensitive, and the group's work was significant. I desperately wanted to do well and was anxious lest the members of the group wouldn't take the content of the session seriously.

So I started the session by sharing the facts. The fact that they all had a lot of experience in their respective fields, that several of them had known me since I had been a newly graduated 20-something with a part-time shop job, that time was short and that someone in authority had imposed this session on them. Then I told them I was nervous, that I was concerned in case their view of me would get in the way of their being able to engage with the activities I had planned and the discussion of the issues at hand, that I felt those discussions were genuinely important if the work they were embarking upon was to be a success. And then I asked them each to say a little about how they were feeling about the session.

I was moved to see just what the impact was of my stating both the facts and my feelings around them. Each of the people in the group shared at a deeper level than I had expected; and more significantly, the scene was set for an afternoon of genuine conversations and all manner of questions, previously lurking in the shadows, were raised, discussed and, for the most part, resolved.

> *Honest disagreement is often a good sign of progress.*
> Mohandas Gandhi (Political and Spiritual Leader)

Deep Conversations: Exercise Ideas

If your aim is to encourage learners to talk at a deeper level, here are nine ideas (in three groups of three) which will facilitate this.

Getting people to talk at a deeper level than simply facts	**Situation One** Learning task when there's an unstated conflict.
	Situation Two Learning task for when all people will express are clichés and platitudes.
	Situation Three Learning task when there is little time for a conversation and issues will need to be returned to.

Situation details, exercise ideas and associated learning points might be:

Situation One	**Talent Show**
Learning task when there's an unstated conflict in a group. (An unstated conflict might be an unspoken grumble from some of the team; a divisive issue that isn't being confronted; a feeling that all is not quite right or some kind of behaviour that some of a group consider unacceptable but aren't addressing to the rest of the group.)	After any task, or with an established team, take two of the group to one side and ask them to take the role of talent show judges in the mould of Simon Cowell (or equivalent). Ask the judges to give feedback to each of the other participants on their current contribution and then to hold up score cards (one to five) to rate their colleagues' performance. Alternatively, and potentially more explosively, require them to decide (yes or no) if they want each of their colleagues to be their teammate in the next activity. They must say no at least once or twice. Rotate the judging panel so everyone gets a turn.
	Zoo's Who?
	Get the group embody their group as a Zoo or a Noah's Ark. (Provide pictures or children's toys if appropriate). Have the group decide which individual animals make up the team at that moment. Perhaps allow each individual to pick one for themselves and have the rest of the group pick one for them. When an individual labels himself as a lion, and the group badge him a warthog, there's sure to be a conversation of some sort.

Situation One continued	**Barriers to Excellence** Stop the group's discussion and ask: 'What's the one issue that is holding you back from being excellent?' Write each factor on a flipchart and hang the paper on a line stretched from one side of the room to the other (that is, construct a physical barrier to excellence). Have the group discuss ways that the barrier could be metaphorically (and so physically) removed.
Situation Two Learning task for when all people will express are clichés and platitudes.	**Easy Listening** Use your iPod or other music collection. Play an 'easy listening' track to reflect what you're currently hearing. Then play something more challenging and ask the group what they should say to make this the appropriate soundtrack for their discussion.
	Taste Sensation Pause the discussion, and list off a few of the clichés that the group have used. Your objective here is to provoke their irritation. Give every group member a cough sweet to taste. Ask them to describe the product and the experience of consuming it (that is, strong, possibly unpleasant but with good, clarifying intent). Then ask: 'Since clichés are an irritation, what would you say to each other in the current situation that might be like a cough sweet?'
	Interrupt-a-Cliché Give each member of the group a small novelty noise-making toy (for example, kazoo, Swannee whistle, squeaky horn and so on) Insist that any instance of cliché, platitude or management-speak be penalized with an interruptive and obnoxious comedy noise. For instance: 'We need to think outside of the b...' [HONK!!]
Situation Three Learning task when there is little time for a conversation and issues will need to be returned to.	**Snapshot** Give the group a range of words from which to choose – on cards or slips of paper, or 'fridge poetry' magnets. Give them the duration of an egg-timer to silently choose a word they will take on into the next task. Digitally photograph the collection of chosen words as a record to come back to later.
	Sensory Reminder Spritz the room with a room spray. With the fragrance in the room, ask each of the group to write a lesson for themselves on a sticky note. Refresh the scent at a later stage and discuss again. A similar effect could be elicited by appealing to another sense: give out chocolate, play a piece of music, ring a bell, or provide other unique stimuli which can be repeated at a later point.
	Pocket Idea Have a range of small objects available, lots more than members of the group, with some repeats. Ask the group to choose and keep an object that reminds them of something they learned during the last task. The object should be taken and kept in a pocket until you have the opportunity to discuss.

Although the ideas above will provide a starting point for you to create an activity or review an activity for your learners, below there are two fully formed exercises which can be run without alteration.

Getting People Talking (Exercise One) – Magistrate

The aim of this activity is to engage participants in a debate on issues which are relevant to all and yet, at least at the start, removed a little from the training environment.

Note, this exercise can be run with no equipment, and is most comfortable in a space free from furniture: in the open air; in a hall-type room; or with all furniture removed to the sides of the room.

Gather all the participants in the centre of the room and give them a statement such as the ones below. The participants are required to agree or disagree to the statement. 'It depends…' is not allowed at this stage, they must opt for one or the other option.

All participants agreeing with the statement must move to the left of a marked line* on the floor/ground, all those disagreeing must move to the right of it. Example statements that tend to split groups might be:

71 mph on the motorway is a crime.

Crimes of passion are excusable.

'An eye for an eye' is an appropriate penal policy.

Quality is always measurable.

There's no such thing as an accident, it's always someone's fault.

Then move to questions that are more relevant to the topic at hand, such as the following:

It must always be top priority to invest in the team.

Leaders are only as good as the people they lead.

Reflecting on your own effectiveness is the only way to develop.

Change is exciting.

Creativity is an innate ability.

The needs of the organization should take precedence over the needs of the individual.

Clear communication will solve all disputes.

We must always treat people equally.

Some people will resist making a choice, but encourage them to do so. It may be interesting to explore their reticence in a review of this exercise. Then ask the 'yes' group why they agree with the statement, and the 'no' group why they disagree. For some of the questions there will be little scope for debate, but for others the participants will become engaged quickly. As facilitator, encourage (by diverting eye contact and explicit instruction) the differing parties to engage with each other directly. Your role is simply to be the umpire.

Don't allow the debate to continue for any one question for longer than two to three minutes before moving on to the next. Part of the value of this exercise is as an energizer – it is particularly useful for re-engaging a group after a break or to reinvigorate them in a 'slump' time (for example, 2pm on a sunny day after a meal). Five questions is usually sufficient.

The other main benefit of this exercise is that it provides a context for learners to disagree, and to express that disagreement, when the subject at issue is not personal. This affords an opportunity for people to practise some of the communication skills you have introduced (for example, STATE) when their personal stake is not too high.

Review this experience around, for example, how effectively they expressed themselves; what they could have done differently; how they felt about the people who held different views from their own; what influenced their decisions.

Note: * Use masking tape to mark a line on an indoor floor; a loose piece of rope or string will suffice if you are on grass.

Getting People Talking (Exercise Two) – Clear and Coded Communication

This exercise is ostensibly about establishing clear lines of communication and ensuring that all of the team are in full understanding about how the team are communicating. It is also, however, about leadership and the way that a team is managed. If this is something that you want to draw out of the group, then selecting a named leader from the group before the start of the exercise is an option.

Kit required: For each team, a bundle (100+) of ice lolly sticks or (even better) wooden stirrers liberated from a coffee shop.* Pads of paper and pencils and a timing device are also useful.

How many people: Any number from two upwards. Numbers greater than six will require a group split and multiple sets of kit.

Duration: Approximately 30 minutes of activity, not including review.

The set-up: Place a bundle of coffee stirrers on the table in front of each team.

Then, read the following brief (twice) to all the team:

This is an auditory brief which I will read twice. Your time will start when I finish reading for the second time.

Using the kit provided, you must determine a way of communicating with each other without using vocal communication or writing.

This form of communication must be undecipherable to an outside agent.

You have 15 minutes to decide on your shared language. In this time you may write.

After 15 minutes half of the team will be removed and the remaining half will be passed a message by the instructor. They will have five minutes to convert this message into your new shared language and then they will be removed from the exercise. The other half of the team will be invited into the room and will have five minutes to translate the message.

While the team is engaged in learning their language, prepare two messages to be 'translated' and passed on. Note, if the team are new or performing poorly this could be a simple message like 'Coffee is at 11.15' but if the team are established and thriving this could be much more complicated and use far more alphanumeric characters.

After 15 minutes remove half the team and send them out of the room. Give each sub-team a different message and give the 'away' team a new set of wooden sticks.

Give them five minutes to translate the message. Then swap the teams back and ask them to translate the other sub-group's efforts. After five more minutes bring the groups back together and ask them to reveal their translations.

Note: * Often training venues have bundles of these, which is where this exercise originated from. Dry spaghetti would also work here.

This exercise works well for a number of reasons. As an introduction to a communication session it sets up and primes a huge number of issues for the trainer. As part of (for example) a team away day, it's a fun, but serious way of getting groups problem-solving and thinking about the way that they currently communicate. It also has potential for existing expertises to come out (for example, if someone understands semaphore or another code). In addition, it requires that groups plan properly for the second phase of the exercise where teams are separated. This makes it a great exercise if you are working with project teams who are geographically separated.

How well people communicate with one another is influenced by a massive number of factors. However, possibly the most important of these is how individuals perceive others and how they themselves are perceived. The diversity of individuals, the associated perceptions and the issues that can arise from this situation will be addressed in the following chapter.

CHAPTER 10 *Exploring Diversity Issues*

Diversity: the art of thinking independently together.

Malcolm Forbes (Publisher)

The Need for Understanding

There can be no organizations that are not aware of the changing employment climate, migratory workforce, drivers for compliance with Equality and Disability Discrimination legislation, aging population and the huge number of other factors which shape the way that they now recruit, train, treat and promote their employees.[1] Yet these issues are often not *fully* addressed, out of reticence or even fear, on the part of the organization or on the part of the individual trainer or manager. The hugely important issues around diversity have become so loaded with the burden of political correctness that often we either don't know how to raise them directly, or we feel that we can't. The chosen solution here is often for organizations to tell their people about their 'policies' and how these relate to the law, but this doesn't address the issue at hand, merely it provides corporate lip service to doing the 'right thing'.

The real 'right' thing here is not to present corporate policy, but to truly engage with one simple issue: people are different, so deal with it.

People *are* different. How they look, sound, move around, and how they operate both inside and outside the workplace – all of these factors and more can vary. When we review an experience in order to optimize the learning, often a powerful question is asked: What could you do differently? Imagine what we could learn in terms of alternative ways of approaching the challenges we meet, if we could truly enhance our appreciation and understanding of the differences between people.

As a trainer it took me a long time to get to grips with the issue of people being different, as I felt uncomfortable raising it from a position of ignorance. I am after all white, heterosexual, grew up somewhere in the middle class and spent many privileged years at university. So what insight, I thought, can I possibly provide about diversity or inequality? Yet when I stopped to think properly, I realized that this belief was flawed; of *course* I've been part of a cultural minority. Whenever I travel to new cultures or countries I am in the minority and wonder constantly what the local rules of the game are. Whenever my partner invites colleagues to dinner, I am torn by the dilemma of whether, since I am in the minority, I should conform to their ways and listen to their office politics all night or whether I should assert my sense of self.

---

1   This chapter, and the materials within, are intended in no way to be construed as meeting any legal compliance with Equality and Employment Law of any type, and is most certainly not to be confused with legal advice. In case of any doubt with regard to organizational policy, or regional and national law, the appropriate counsel should be sought. The authors take no responsibility for actions taken based on the contents herein.

Once we realize that we all have experience of being in the minority, of being 'other' in some way, we start to lose the paralysis of political correctness and treat people as people regardless. Then we can genuinely embrace the notion that if we don't engage with this issue we run the risk of losing a huge amount of richness and perhaps strength from the way a group, team or organization could perform.

By reviewing our experience, we also begin to understand not just the intellectual or legal issues, but also the human response to being in the minority. In a powerful and sometimes uncomfortable sense, the experience helps us to learn both from the observed difference in others and from actually being different ourselves.

Practitioner's Enquiries

On what occasions have you ever been in a 'minority' group? (Or a cultural outsider?) What were the feelings and thoughts that you associated with that experience?*

How much did your minority position affect your performance and alter your ability to function effectively?

Note: * This needn't be anything lasting…it could be as simple as your first day in a new job, at someone else's family gathering or travelling overseas by yourself.

In addition, as trainers and facilitators within learning organizations, if we are to truly deal with diversity issues then perhaps we need to examine our own practices before we seek to educate others. After all, as Hutchinson and Bromley (2007) note:

Until our thinking breaks away from an image of standard [learners] attending short courses and truly embraces the diversity of our population and the possibilities of a myriad of delivery vectors, we will never achieve the cultural change to which we aspire.

There is of course an inherent tension involved in providing any form of training or facilitation; and that is that what is normal and expected for one group may well be abnormal, unexpected and possibly unacceptable to another. So, the issues discussed in this chapter, perhaps more than any other chapter, require people to truly understand other perspectives in order to learn from them. This understanding may come from sharing of information in the form of honest and open communication; but the experiencing of the other perspectives will enrich it. It is this deep understanding which will truly change organizational cultures – not forced action to comply with a change in legislation.

Diverse Diversity

Diversity can come in many forms; people differ in their nationality, ethnicity, gender, race, religious belief, sexual orientation, abilities, health, age and in many other ways. From a training and development perspective, *The Equal Opportunities Handbook* (Clements and Spinks, 2000) gives a very good overview of the key issues at play. However, this chapter is not concerned with the legal compliance issues that surround direct and indirect discrimination, victimization and harassment in the workplace; and since most institutions of size have their own in-house team of lawyers and special advisors, it is likely that the diversity with which you will be most overtly dealing is around cultural diversity and equality issues. As such we've written the chapter from that perspective. However, the tools, techniques and ideas that we present are entirely transferable to other forms of workplace diversity.

> *All the people like us are we, and everyone else is They.*
>
> Rudyard Kipling (Writer)

A long time ago I ran a day-long interactive creativity session for a group of Chinese engineers. The delegates were extremely polite, very clever, and when asked to solve problems they were innovative and insightful. However, no matter what I tried I couldn't get them to discuss process or engage with anything that wasn't purely task-based. On matters that weren't immediately familiar they looked at me agog and deferred to my wisdom. As such I ended up 'teaching' instead of facilitating their learning. My questions fell flat, my enquiries died on the vine and my well-conceived programme was flailing dismally. I remember sending a text message to a colleague at the lunch break reporting that I thought that I was dying a slow death. However, at the end of the session they clapped, said how useful the session had been and individually came and thanked me profusely for my contributions. Far from being pleased by this result, I drove home that night fuming about how 'they could have shown some of that enthusiasm in the morning' and other dark mutterings.

Much of the supposed benefit of the intervention was based on my assumptions, values and understanding of what was 'normal' behaviour. I'd expected contributions and discussions around the process, as well as the task. They'd expected me to be in charge and tell them how to do things. On reflection I learned valuable lessons that day about my agenda as a facilitator as well as the cultural workings of other people.

Throughout this book, we've presented a style of learning, working and thinking as being a good or better way of being. We stand by our philosophies – but they're not right – just different from other ways (both cultural and academic) of approaching training and development.

So before starting to design, construct and facilitate a learning experience around diversity issues it is worth spending a little time considering the way in which beliefs, values and assumptions will impact upon your facilitation when it comes to the issue in question. For instance, the following questions might prove useful.

Practitioner's Enquiries

When in a minority situation, how much does your own personality affect how much you respect the majority norm and fit in or maintain your sense of self?

What is your own cultural/racial/gender/ethnic/religious background?

What do you consider to be 'normal' behaviour and what do you take for granted?

How do your norms differ from the people with whom you work?

> What are the behaviours that you see in your participants that particularly irritate or disturb you? Are these behaviours objectively unacceptable; or do they stem from a cultural expectation?

Before designing your session or exercise, you need also to understand why any intervention is necessary in the first place. Is it to satisfy some organizational or legal driver at induction? Have issues arisen that have led to management deciding that some sort of external event is required? Is it simply a desire on the part of a leader to have their team more fully aware of each other to push performance to a new level? Has there been a change of team? Is it simply an intervention required to help people understand the norms of the (professional and wider) culture in which they now find themselves?

I'd also make a special effort to discover *where* in the organization the intervention is expected to have an impact; since diversity issues can arise prior to an individual's employment (in the form of job adverts and descriptors, and at selection and interview), during employment (in the form of access to development, promotion, trainings and harassment) and after employment (in the form of redundancy procedures, exit interviews and references).

Additionally, if the organization in which you are working is *truly* embracing diversity as an issue, you may want to consider if and how any ideas and thoughts raised in the meeting or session can be passed back up the organizational chain and perhaps effect some change (however small) at all levels.

Practitioner's Enquiries

What is the reason for your intervention? (Legal compliance at induction, remedial dealing with problematic issue and so on.)

Is the perceived driver chiefly a legal, moral, ethical or performance-based one?

What would be the benefits to the individuals in question, the people as a collective, the task performance, any other stakeholders and the organization as a whole if the issues were explored or resolved?

How else has the organization, as a whole, addressed this issue?

How have other facets of the same organization (with maybe similar values and norms) addressed similar issues?

Where will your intervention sit chronologically with relation to an individual's relationship with the organization? (First day; established team; and so on.)

To what extent can any issue raised during any diversity intervention be reported (and perhaps embraced and implemented) within the organization as a whole?

The Meaning of Diversity

Since, as a facilitator, I need to resolve clearly in my mind is what *type* of diversity is to be explored, it's probably worth having the learners undergo those same enquiries. In the type of activities relayed here the type of agenda is a cultural one, but it might equally be racial, gender, religious and so on. This issue can be explored with both practical and discursive approaches; and here are two ideas to get you thinking.

Practical Exercise Idea – The Meaning of Diversity

Ask small groups of participants to 'go and find 25 objects that represent diversity.' Give them 15–20 minutes to consider and collect. On their return, have them explain the thinking behind their scavenged collection.

Discursive Exercise Idea – The Meaning of Diversity

Set up a number of flipchart stations around the room. Write a question related to diversity at the top of each flipchart and issue each participant with a pack of sticky notes. Ask that the participants walk around the room writing thoughts, issues or ideas from each station on to their sticky note and placing it on the relevant chart. After an appropriate period have the group divide themselves amongst the flipcharts and act as creative consultants in how to solve the various issues presented. After an appropriate time they should then present their solutions back to the group as a whole. (You may wish to apply some of the creativity techniques as discussed in Chapter 7.) The intent here is partly to raise the issue, and partly to foster safe environment where everyone can contribute.

The type of questions that you may wish to use are:

In this organization, what is the meaning of diversity? Is it right?

How can we use peoples' differences to greater effect?

Where could we make this organization more inclusive?

Regarding diversity and equality, where does this organization say one thing and do another?

How could this organization more effectively recruit, train, employ and promote individuals from minority groups?

Legal Compliance or Excellent Performance?

Laws control the lesser man...Right conduct controls the greater one.

Mark Twain (Writer)

Often the issues surrounding equality and diversity in the workplace form part of an institutions' corporate programme of induction. Certainly I have sat through essentially the same PowerPoint slides about corporate responsibility to the workforce on a number of occasions at a number of institutions. If you haven't sat through that same presentation, take a look at your corporate marketing brochure or your campus prospectus. I'm betting that people of all shapes, sizes, ethnicities and abilities will be fully represented.

As a society, particularly in the UK, we have made progress over the last few decades in addressing many of the very serious issues around institutional discrimination; yet on a local level the small unspoken differences between people, especially cultural ones, are the issues that as a facilitator of individual learning you may be best placed to address quickly.

The bottom line here is that legal compliance is not the same as excellent performance. Compliance with legislation may modify behaviour; but understanding will change attitudes and thus allow learning to take place. And learning leads to excellent performance.

Differences challenge assumptions.

Anne Wilson Schaef (Writer and Lecturer)

Diversity of Values and Beliefs

Cultures are shaped by what people value and the beliefs that they hold about the world. Often these values and beliefs are powerful (see the Chapter 4 in this book regarding leadership values), and if misunderstood by others can result in considerable tension or worse. Countries and cultures, after all, go to war over their beliefs and resultant actions.

In Chapter 7 we discussed the Ladder of Inference and its value to the creative facilitator. The tool's value is highly pronounced in the case of helping teams to explore diversity issues, namely:

We treat people inappropriately (action)
Our actions are driven by our (inaccurate) beliefs
Our inaccurate beliefs are derived from our (flawed) conclusions
Our conclusions are founded on (ignorant) assumptions
Our assumptions are based around confused meanings
Our meanings come from narrow and selective data

Our particular value system drives all of these stages and so interventions based around the different values which different individuals from different cultures hold. Here are three exercise ideas that can help to quickly open up discussions of values.

Diversity Values and Beliefs Exercise Idea One

Give the group a bag including:

A coin	A teabag	A candle
A book	A postcard of modern art	A raffle ticket

Or any items which could be considered valuable to some and not to others, and valuable in a range of ways. For instance, a teabag has little financial value however 'a cup of tea' represents friendship, stability and tranquility.

Ask the group to rank them in terms of priority, most to least valuable.

(Alternatively pictures of these items can be substituted to represent arts, commerce, experience, wisdom or heritage and so on.)

Debrief around the differences between individuals and where those originate from.

Diversity Values and Beliefs Exercise Idea Two

Have the group produce a survival guide to working and being successful in the organization, which will be read by new employees.

Have them produce different chapters, pages or sections that will be sent to different cultures or countries.

Diversity Values and Beliefs Exercise Idea Three

Have the group produce a marketing brochure, focusing on the attributes of the organization valued by different cultural group. Such activities can also get at issues surrounding Appearance and Dress if appropriate.

Simulating Diversity, Equality and Inequality

At its most simple, inequality of any sort is essentially about a reduction of opportunities. In an experiential learning setting, reduction of opportunity is easy to achieve; by taking an equal group and making them in some way unequal:

- By artificially depriving certain members of a specific sense (and insisting that *all* members are treated equally and participate equally) opens up huge territories of debates around the treatment of people in the workplace who are in some way differently abled. By briefing or doing an exercise in a way that some of the group can't access, you can simulate many cultural issues.

- By excluding certain team members from certain roles within a task you can simulate issues around any sort of equality or inequality with which you wish to draw a parallel. It can be as simple as singling out the people who are brown-haired and taking them to one side for two minutes while the rest of the blonde, grey, red and black-haired group start to define the roles that they will take. The minority group is then at a disadvantage, and with skilful review this can be easily equated to workplace or other forms of inequality.
- By issuing a briefing in a language that some of the group speak fluently and some do not, you immediately simulate the exact situation faced by huge numbers of employees in this country every day. This can be amplified if the briefing contains culturally specific references to which all members of the group are not privy.

Each of these tactics is explored with the fully formed exercises and ideas which follow. However, again the key to success in this area is the review and not the task. In some ways the area of inequality and diversity is the easiest one in which to design an activity or adapt an existing one (by changing the rules or conditions to suit some and not others). The review, however, is potentially the hardest type for a facilitator. These are not trivial issues, and real skill is needed to ensure the parallels are clear and participants do not feel that important concerns are being treated flippantly.

For instance, I ran a teambuilding event a couple of years ago, and over coffee I'd been speaking to an employee who seemed to be fairly disenfranchised and had been passed over for a number of promotions. My interpretation was that she believed there was something more to her predicament than just her quality of performance, but she had not stated *explicitly* that she was being discriminated against. Rather than delve further, or contrive to turn a group conversation to it, I decided to alter the next exercise (a typical newspaper bridge construction-type task) and quickly made some briefing tickets. I silently passed these to *some* team members and started the task. The tickets said that the bearer was forbidden from using their strong hand (so left-handed people were forced to use their right only) for the duration of the task. This caused issues and problems with the task, and afterwards I asked them how they felt to have been hampered in this manner. I followed this discussion with another question about whether such situations arose in the workplace for them for real, but instead of dialoguing with the full group I asked that they go for a walk in pairs and return in a few minutes having discussed that question. When they all returned, it was clear that *some* of the pairs had had quite emotional conversations, and we then spent a long time unpacking the issues, and helping the team and management start to address what was being thought but not spoken.

Some conflicts arise not from major, obvious cultural differences, but from unrecognised minor ones.

Sivasailan 'Thiagi' Thiagarajan (Educator and Writer)

Diversity of Professional Attitudes

Our attitudes affect our behaviour. It could be argued that, in terms of sheer professionalism, it is the behaviour that is significant – it doesn't matter if I don't like someone, providing I behave towards that person with courtesy. It is also true that I perform most productively in the workplace with those colleagues with whom I have a relationship based not on mere professional tolerance but on mutual understanding and respect. It is through these relationships that I am able to learn and develop in the light of the differences between us. Of course, it is also probably true that no amount of away days and courses are going to create life-long friendships in people if that is not naturally occurring.

Practitioner's Questions

How have you noticed people from different cultures engaging with your place of work?

What are the general rules of engagement by which people in your organization are expected to play? From where do these rules originate?

What difference do personality and culture make to the way that people around you relate to their seniors and juniors, authority figures and the professional norms of the institution?

Many years ago, a German researcher came on an exchange programme to work in the department where I was completing my PhD. After a couple of days of work at the bench he asked why a key procedure was being carried out in the manner that we all used. 'That's just the way we do it here,' we told him. This fuzziness of thought clearly troubled him, because later he came and spoke to us individually. 'But it's ridiculous to do it like that,' he told us and then pointed out how it could be done more efficiently. He was absolutely correct, and yet we were still using the old technique long after he'd gone back to his home research institute. Everyone agreed that it was inefficient, and no one knew who had decided on that particular method in the first place, but that was how things happened here and we weren't keen to change. The story is not a unique event. Any localized groups can become entrenched in their own, almost tribal, practices, which can frequently go unchallenged.

In organizations, majority groups will define what is 'normal'. This is not to suggest intolerance of any sort, but 'that's just the way we do it here' is a powerful force to be reckoned with, regardless of any legal, ethical or moral pressure. If the majority group defines what is normal, protects their own traditions, and imposes their own values onto a process, department or organization, then it is clear that any differences between the majority and minority group can be inadvertently exaggerated and stereotypes maintained.

Practitioner's Enquiries

What are the unspoken and unwritten rules of engagement in the/your department?

What is the norm in the/your organization?

In an exponentially changing world, are those norms acceptable?

If you could change just one thing about the way diversity issues are handled within your institution, what would have the greatest impact?

For us, *the* classic experiential learning game in the area of norms and attitudes is 'Barnga'; an elegant and simple cultural simulation exercise where rules and norms of simulated organizations affect the new members of said organizations in potentially very powerful ways. It's certainly worth owning a copy! The thinking and methods *behind* the exercise, however, offer a creative trainer a wealth of possible material. By giving two or more groups of people different 'rules' for an exercise, embedding those rules, and then in some way recombining those sub-groups (and limiting process discussion or providing a strong task-based focus) the cultural norms of the groups can clash in interesting ways. This opens up vast scope for learning.

Norms, Beliefs and Workplace Attitudes Exercise Ideas

In your exercise designs, could you simulate 'normal' behaviour by instilling certain different rules for different people and then bringing them together?

These rules might be subtle variants on each other to simulate mild cultural friction or could be in complete opposition with each other to simulate huge culture shock. This can be complex and involved, or very quick and simple.

For instance: divide your group into two teams and separate them so they cannot communicate with each other. Give out a written brief which requires that both teams have to learn and perfect a simple game. This game should be something simple (akin to 'noughts and crosses') but provide different rules to each team (for example, one team gets the normal rules and one team gets a rule that says, 'You can place two crosses for every nought played'). Then recombine the teams. The frustration, annoyance and confusion that result can seed a huge amount of discussion and provide energy and focus to a more formal session.

As a workable concept, this idea might take on the following form:

Exercise Idea – Playground Game Strategy

Separate the group into two and issue both teams with a pile of red, green and blue milk-bottle tops and a written brief (as with 'Barnga' a little bit of deceptive theatre leading to an assumption that the briefs are both the same can go a long way here) containing the following type of information:

'You have five minutes to learn the rules to this child's playground game and as a team perfect a foolproof winning strategy. In front of you there are three types of counters and these each have a different value. The game itself must be played in silence. Each player must hold three counters under the table: one red, one green, one blue; and must choose one of the counters to play. On the trainer's command,'one, two, three, draw!' each player must place their chosen counter on the table. This must be done instantly and your opponent must do the same. The colour you choose, in relation to your opponent's colour, decides who wins the bout and who loses.

[Differing brief – give only to team one] red beats blue, beats green, beats red.

[Differing brief – give only to team two] green beats blue, beats red, beats green.

After the bout concludes you must decide *in silence* who won that round. You then have 30 seconds silently, and without communicating with your opponent, to plan your approach for the next round where the process will be repeated. Draws count as no points for either player, and the first player to seven victories wins.'

Exercise Variations

As a variant on the game you could brief a third group of participants as 'prefects' who have the job to call 'one, two, three, draw' and then silently and unquestionably adjudicate who has won or lost. Their brief could differ again (for example, 'red counters always win' – which would confuse *both* players) or their brief could be the same as one team's and different from the other's so they always side with one team. This is a potentially valuable twist on the set-up as it simulates institutional prejudice and makes the issue of 'it doesn't matter what we did, we always lose' into something that is very tangible very quickly.

As usual, the strength or value here only really comes from the debrief questions, and so you may want to follow the following lines of enquiry:

Possible debrief questions.

  What interesting issues did this raise?

  How did it feel when *your* rules weren't adhered to?

  In the light of ambiguous information, what factors decided who won each bout? (This question forms a neat segue into personality versus cultural norms and adherence).

  (If the biased prefect strategy was employed) How did it feel to be championed when you lost or discriminated against when you won?

How is this like a real organizational situation?

What are the unspoken/unwritten rules of this organization?

Diversity of Communication and Language

Cultural barriers can be very simple language-based ones; from linguistic misunderstandings to the situations that arise when a reference, word or gesture means different things to different people. This is a constant issue for the roving consultant and I have to check my assumptions regularly when working in different countries and organizations. A shake of the head, for instance, doesn't always mean what I think it does. So how could an exercise explore these types of issues? Here are some ideas to get your creativity flowing.

Communication and Language Exercise – Idea One

Whilst doing any existing task,* issues of communication can be simulated by depriving certain individuals of a key sense (sight, sound, touch). Briefing a group on a task while another member is absent will also have this effect.

Debrief around what actual barriers the team face in reality.

Note: * Either ones you create yourself, ones from this book, from the additional resources listed at the back, or ones that you've bought but have gone stale.

Communication and Language Exercise – Idea Two

Presenting an instruction to the group in a foreign language that you know some will understand and most will not.

I once ran a bonding session for a team comprising a mix of nationalities. I ensured that all task instructions were written with each paragraph in a different language and some key information presented in Roman numerals, binary code and other non-shared decipherable languages. This was presented as problem-solving material, but was actually about the group having to rely on each other and trust the information each was giving.

Debrief around whether the group really share a language that they all fully understand.

Idea Communication and Language Exercise – Idea Three

'When I do X, it means Y.'

To illustrate the notion that language is not all spoken, you could ask the individuals in a group to think of a novel, unique and personal gesture/pose for emotions and stances such as fear, euphoria, pride, sad, happy, nausea, anger and so on. Limit your list of gestures to five and display the words on a flipchart.

Stand the group up in space and then read out some words like:

Britain	Family	Festival
School	Bananas	Politician
'This Team'	Jazz/Modern Art	Childhood

Then ask each member to make the appropriate gesture and posture for that word. The rest of the group have to guess their colleagues' feelings or thoughts from their gestures alone.

Debrief around what assumptions or misrepresentations happen in the workplace.

Diversity of Cultural and Personal Needs

In any team, each individual will certainly have needs, drivers and beliefs that are personal to them, or culturally shared. What is also highly likely is that sometimes these will, in some way, be at odds with those expected within their organization. Some years ago, for example, as a university teacher, I sat in heated meetings discussing how we should handle the needs of students who had continually to absent themselves from certain key Friday classes to go and pray.

Practitioner's Enquiries

What in your life is non-negotiable insofar as you are concerned?

What personal rights would you, if they were compromised, resign over?

Which of these issues are personal to you and which come from belonging to a larger grouping of people (whether a family, culture, non-work organization or religion)?

What potential conflicts can you identify between these issues and beliefs and the way that an employer might expect you to behave 'professionally' and in accordance with their practices and protocols?

Often the difference in treatment or expectations of individuals by organizations can be a very real source of friction – either between the organization and individual (as in the case above) or between individuals themselves. These issues don't necessarily need to be major cultural markers to be worthy of discussion. Recently I was facilitating a team away day, and the pivotal moment of the day, to which nearly every other instance of friction was linked, was when the non-smokers objected to the special dispensation and break arrangements that the company provided for the smokers. Here are a couple of exercise ideas that can open up discussion of cultural and personal need.

Cultural and Personal Need Exercise Idea One

Midway through any experiential task remove a key member of the group for five minutes, and then reintroduce them.

Alternatively, issue a secret written instruction to one or more team members that at a certain time they must leave without explaining the reason for five minutes and then reappear, similarly with no explanation.

Debrief around what feelings this provoked in the absented individual and the rest of the team; the issues of personal need (cultural, family, religious) versus institutional commitments; and what dialogue might be required within the team to ensure that everyone is comfortable with arrangements and feels that they are being treated with equity.

Cultural and Personal Need Exercise Idea Two

Teams are often tasked by trainers to talk and find common ground or interesting similarities. Yet, in the words of Aristotle, 'The worst form of inequality is to try to make unequal things equal.' So why not have them amplify and celebrate their differences? Have them find issues that split the group (two or more people holding one opinion, the rest holding another). In ten minutes, have them find 30 ways in which they are different to each other (once they exhaust the obvious ten or 15, they'll struggle, and this struggle will produce the interesting material).

Review around which of those issues are ones which can help the team to become excellent and which are the most problematic. You may wish to have them 'Get at the Honesty' here – see Part II of this book.

Often this type of exercise can also act as a precursor to conflict resolution trainings. It may be worth re-reading Chapter 9 'Getting People Talking' to consider how you'd deal with this issue.

Cultural and Personal Need Exercise Idea Three

Using marketing and brochure materials to establish the cultural mix of your organization (and your HR division's diversity statistics to mitigate against assumptions), hand over the catering budget for the day to the group and ask the them to plan and buy the components of a meal that a representative group can share *without compromise*.

This exercise works effectively because it relies not only on racial, cultural and religious diversity but also on personal conviction (for example, vegetarian, ethical sourcing, additive-free preferences).

Sense of Self and Personal Space

Many experiential activities have an element of physicality to them, and culturally this can sometimes pose problems or make a poorly thought-through design impossible for some learners. This can, on the other hand, force a diversity conversation very quickly.

Recently I was acting as an instructor on a corporate leadership day on a high-ropes course. One of the challenges was to cross a simulated river using a variety of ropes, barrels and planks. The team I was with had, from a distance, watched other groups doing the exercise, and had realized that most groups were holding on to each other and generally becoming quite intimate in order to carry out the task successfully. As we walked to the exercise, one member of my group quietly told me that she wouldn't be able to do the next part of the course as her belief system prevented her from physical contact of this nature. I thought that this was a good opportunity to explore diversity and leadership issues. I asked the group to choose a leader, and then asked to leader to spend time planning around the team and individuals' needs *before* they even mentioned ropes, barrels and buckets. In this conversation the issue of personal space came up, and the participant asked if the leader could excuse her from the task. I stepped in and insisted that no participant should do anything with which they were uncomfortable, but they *must make an equal contribution to the success of the task*. As a group they discussed how the various needs of the situation could be met, and arrived at an elegant solution which met all the criteria, including consideration of the cultural sensitivities in the group and the insistence of equality. It proved to be a powerful moment for the group, and following on from that event they improved noticeably in their performances as their future planning was built around the individual and team needs, not just purely on the task.

In any exercise, stressing and insisting upon an *equal contribution from all* can allow a group to realize and explore diversity issues.

Personal Space Exercise Idea – How Close is Too Close?

If you are working with an international group, a simple way to powerfully experience the difference between cultures is to place people into two lines, facing each other. Try to ensure that the individuals facing each other are from different national or cultural backgrounds.

Ask first one line, and then the other, to take a step forward, towards their partner. Stop at the limit of comfort. Then notice when one partner would be comfortable a step closer than their partner. How does this feel?

Review around the difference, how the comfortable distance reflects the culture, how it feels to be 'invaded' or 'repelled'.

In a UK setting, this has the advantage that those in the cultural majority, those with white British backgrounds, are likely to be amongst those feeling uncomfortable first.

The strategy behind this technique can be adapted to explore how some behaviours are acceptable to some and unacceptable to others, or even to bring into sharp relief issues concerning workplace harassment.

Relationships, Roles and Responsibilities

We find our identity through our relationship with another.

Richard Rohr (Spiritual Writer)

Different cultural backgrounds within the workplace mean that individuals view their roles, relationships and responsibilities, not to mention rewards and recognitions, in different ways. Some of these views are amplified, often inaccurately, by cultural stereotypes. Before you ask a group to experientially understand diversity you may have need to consider the way that different cultures interact with:

Authority	Management
Leadership	Followership
Gender	Teachers
Learning	Work-life balance

As such any task or idea that we've presented in this book can be used to access and explore cultural differences. To return to the opening premise of this chapter, people are different – so deal with it. Here's a final exercise to help you explore just *how* different the people within an organization can be.

Diversity Exercise Idea – The Same But Different

This exercise requires multiple (at least 50–100) items that are identical in some ways and different in others. If these objects can be easily connected or joined in some way, this is a definite advantage. The types of objects you may consider are one of the following or equivalent: coloured plastic or wooden children's building blocks, different colours of modelling clay or coloured paperclips.

Lay the pile of objects out on the table and ask a small group of participants to use them to explain and describe diversity in all its forms within the organization. In short, how are the employees in the organization *the same but different*?

At first glance, this seems like a very simple premise, but it quickly becomes enormously complicated, as our assumptions, beliefs and understandings are challenged. The similarity of the objects as a metaphor for employees, the differences between the objects to represent diversity, and the connectivity of the objects to represent team and organization can all stimulate conversation and open up discussion about what an all-encompassing issue diversity can be.

As Gregory Bateson, the noted anthropologist once asserted: 'Learning proceeds from difference.' Where experience can raise awareness of difference and the opportunities that difference provides, real learning can take place and difference can be celebrated.

11 *Final Thoughts and Last Words*

Experience is the teacher of all things.

Julius Caesar (Roman Emperor)

Recently I visited a remote island in the North Atlantic. I reached it in a small boat and for most of the four-hour outward voyage I was standing, enjoying the wildlife and the sensation of pitching with the ocean's swell. When the time came to disembark, I knew, intellectually, that there could be a physical effect of having stood for so long at sea. I only remembered this as one of my co-travellers stumbled when he took his first faltering steps on terra firma. But it was when *I* stepped out of the boat and on to the quayside that I really understood what it meant to have altered balance and what the negative implications of this could be. I felt it; I remember it; and it will change the way I carry fragile items forever.

In this book we have presented a range of facilitation challenges. How can you facilitate learning about teamwork, leadership, personal effectiveness, change, creativity, organizational quality, communication or diversity with limited resources? How is it possible for people to learn about these areas in a limited period of time? Our argument is that an experience, whether or not that experience is 'artificial', will evoke an emotion and the learning that can come from this emotional response will have a long-lasting impact.

We have provided a number of ideas for artificial experiences; and we hope that you will find these useful. But more than this, we hope that you will enter in to the creative facilitation process by designing, developing and adapting artificial experiential learning activities for the people you are working with. Creative facilitation is not for someone else. It's for you.

To you, Baldrick, the Renaissance was just something that happened to other people, wasn't it?
Edmund Blackadder mocks his dogsbody.
Blackadder the Second BBC TV

As is evident throughout, this book is a joint venture. However, it is not just in the writing that we have come together – the collaboration has not been one of simply editing each other's work and agreeing content. The best of the exercises, both the fully formed ones and the ideas, are the ones on which we have worked together. Both of us can, and do, develop perfectly adequate learning activities alone; however the exercises are more robust, and the process more enjoyable, when we are able to share the creative process.

If you do not already participate in a like-minded network within which you can co-create, we would suggest that you explore possibilities to do this.

The list of acknowledgements at the start of the book is comprised of people who have been with us through the journey into creative facilitation, from (and with) whom we have learned. Everyone who is on this journey will be aware of the necessity to practise what we impress upon our learners: try something; review the results; adapt as appropriate; and do it again. If you make the time and space to review your activities from a facilitation perspective, both your training and your interventions more generally will have increased rigour and verve.

How wonderful it is that nobody need wait a single moment before starting to improve the world.
Anne Frank (Diarist)

Be courageous in your design. Be playful. Be inventive. Be true to your own facilitative style. But beyond any of these, be sure that whatever you do, say or create has learning at the centre. Because if you have the learning of your participants at the heart of what you are engaged in, there is no such thing as limited resources.

Bibliography

Preface: Why Read this Book and How to Use It

Highmore Simms, N. (2006) *How to Run a Great Workshop* Pearson: Prentice-Hall Business.

Part I: The Concept of Experiential Learning

CHAPTER 1   OPTIMIZING ARTIFICIAL EXPERIENTIAL LEARNING

De Bono, E. (1990, Originally 1970) *Lateral Thinking* Penguin.

Fry, H., Ketteridge, S. and Marshall, S. (1999) *A Handbook of Teaching and Learning in Higher Education – Enhancing Academic Practice* (Chapter 3 Understanding Student Learning) Kogan Page.

Hardingham, A. (1998) *Psychology for Trainers* IPD.

Honey, P. and Mumford, A. (1982) *The Manual of Learning Styles* (Published in 1982, 1986 and 1992; discontinued in 2000) Replaced by *Learning Styles Questionnaire and Learning Styles Helper's Guide*. See http://www.peterhoney.com for more information.

Knight, S. (1995) *Neuro-Linguistic Programming at Work* Nicholas Brearley Publishing.

Kolb, D. (1984) *Experiential Learning: Experience as the Source of Learning and Development* Prentice Hall.

Part II: The Skills of Facilitation

CHAPTER 2   EXTRACTING THE LESSON: HOW TO REVIEW, CAPTURE AND AMPLIFY LEARNING

Adair, J. (2006 2nd Edition) *Leadership and Motivation* Kogan Page.

Alder, A. (2010) *Pattern Making Pattern Breaking* Gower Publishing.

Ancona, D. and Isaacs, W. (2006) *Structural Balance of Teams [4 Player Model]* in *Exploring Positive Relationships at Work: Building a Theoretical and Research Foundation* (Dutton and Ragins, eds., 2006) Psychology Press.

Clements, P. and Spinks, T. (1993) *A Practical Guide to Facilitation Skills: A Real-World Approach* Kogan Page.

Gerrickens, P. (1998) *The Feedback Game* Gower Publishing.

Kantor, D. and Lehr, W. (1975) *Inside the Family* Jossey-Bass.

Kraybill, R. (1994) Facilitating Facilitation. *The Child Care Worker*, Vol.12, No.7, p.13.

Landale, A. and Douglas, M. (2002) *The Fast Facilitator* Gower Publishing.

Patterson, K., Grenny, J., McMillan, R. and Switzler, A. (2002) *Crucial Conversations: Tools for Talking When the Stakes are High* McGraw Hill.

Schwarz, R. (2002) *The Skilled Facilitator* Jossey-Bass.

Scott, S. (2003) *Fierce Conversations* Piatkus Books.

Stone, D., Patton, B. and Heen, S. (1999) *Difficult Conversations* Penguin Publishing.

Part III: The Developer's Toolbox – Specific Issues and Tactics

CHAPTER 3   HELPING TEAMS WORK

Luft, J. (1969) *Of Human Interaction: The Johari Model* Mayfield Publishing Co.

Tuckman, B. (1965) Developmental Sequence in Small Groups. *Psychological Bulletin,* Vol.63, p.384–399.

CHAPTER 4   FACILITATING LEADERSHIP DEVELOPMENT

Adair, J. (2005) *How to Grow Leaders* Kogan Page.

Adair, J. (2006 2nd Edition) *Leadership and Motivation* Kogan Page.

Goffee, R. and Jones, G. (2006) *Why Should Anyone be Led By You?* Harvard Business School Press.

Kotter, J.P. (1996) *Leading Change* Harvard Business School Press.

Kouzes, J.M. and Posner, B.Z. (2007 4th Edition) *The Leadership Challenge* Jossey-Bass.

Owen, J. (2005) *How to Lead* Pearson Education Limited.

CHAPTER 5   BUILDING PERSONAL EFFECTIVENESS

Briggs-Meyers, I. and Meyers, P. (1980) *Gifts Differing* Davies-Black Publishing.

Carnegie, D. (2006 New Edition) *How to Win Friends and Influence People* Vermillion Publishing.

Covey, S.R. (2004 2nd Edition) *Seven Habits of Highly Effective People* Simon and Schuster UK Ltd.

Doran, G.T. (1981) There's a S.M.A.R.T. Way to Write Management's Goals and Objectives. *Management Review*, Vol.70, No.11.

Gleeson, K. (2004 3rd Edition) *The Personal Efficiency Program: How to Get Organized to Do More Work in Less Time* John Wiley and Sons.

Goleman, D. (1996) *Emotional Intelligence* Bloomsbury Publishing.

Goleman, D. (1999) *Working With Emotional Intelligence* Bloomsbury Publishing.

Jaques, D. (1984) *Learning in Groups* Croon Helm.

Salovey, P. and Mayer, J. (1990) Emotional Intelligence. *Imagination, Cognition and Personality,* Vol.9, No.3, pp.185–211.

CHAPTER 6   DEALING WITH CHANGE

Adair, J. (2002) *Inspiring Leadership* Thorogood Publishing.

Barger, N.J. and Kirby, L.K. (1995) *The Challenge of Change in Organizations* Davies-Black Publishing.

CHAPTER 7   PRODUCING CREATIVE AND CRITICAL THINKERS

Allan, D., Kingdon, M., Murrin, K. and Rudkin, D. (1999) *What If? How to Start a Creative Revolution at Work* Capstone Press.

Amabile, T.M. (1996) *Creativity in Context* Westview Press.

Clegg, B. and Birch, P. (2002) *Crash Course in Creativity* Kogan Page.

De Bono, E. (1990, Originally 1970) *Lateral Thinking* Penguin.

De Bono, E. (1997) *How to Be More Interesting* Penguin.

De Bono, E. (2000 edition) *Six Thinking Hats* Penguin.

Dewulf, S. and Baillie, C. (1999) *CASE: How to Foster Creativity* Department for Education and Employment.

Dilts, R.B. (1994) *Strategies of Genius; Volume I* Meta Publications.

Dilts, R.B., Epstein, T. and Dilts, R.W. (1991) *Tools for Dreamers: Strategies for Creativity and the Structure of Innovation* Meta Publications.

Kelley, T. with Littman, J. (2001) *The Art of Innovation* Harper Collins Business.

Michalko, M. (2006 2nd Edition) *Thinkertoys* Ten Speed Press.

Runco, M.A. (2007) *Creativity – Theories and Themes: Research Development and Practice* Elsevier Academic Press.

Senge, P. (1994) *The Fifth Discipline Fieldbook: Strategies for Building a Learning Organization* Nicholas Brearley Publishing.

CHAPTER 8   UNDERSTANDING ORGANIZATIONAL QUALITY

Burlingham, B. (2007) *Small Giants: Companies that Choose to be Great Instead of Big* Penguin Books.

Collard, R. (2006, originally 1989) *Total Quality: Success through People* Jaico Publishing.

Collins, J. (2001) *Good to Great – Why Some Companies Make the Leap and Others Don't* Random House Business Books.

Dawson, S. (1989, first edition 1986) *Analysing Organisations* Macmillan Education.

Haney, C., Banks, C. and Zimbardo, P. (1973) Interpersonal Dynamics in a Simulated Prison. *International Journal of Criminology and Penology*, Vol.1, pp.69–97.

Kirkpatrick, D.L. (1994) *Evaluating Training Programs: The Four Levels* Berrett-Koehler.

Lynch, M. (Devised by) (1991) *Total Quality: An Awareness Building Exercise* Gower Northgate Training.

Waterman Jr, R.H. and Peters, T. (2004 2nd Edition) *In Search Of Excellence: Lessons from America's Best-Run Companies* Profile Business.

CHAPTER 9   GETTING PEOPLE TALKING: BUILDING PRODUCTIVE RELATIONSHIPS

Chambers, J. (1995) *Sociolinguistic Theory: Linguistic Variation and its Social Significance* Blackwell Publishers.

Labov, W. (1972) *Sociolinguistic Patterns* University of Pennsylvania Press.

Patterson, K., Grenny, J., McMillan, R. and Switzler, A. (2002) *Crucial Conversations* McGraw-Hill Publishing.

CHAPTER 10   EXPLORING DIVERSITY ISSUES

Clements, P. and Spinks, T. (2000 3rd Edition) *The Equal Opportunities Handbook* Kogan Page.

Hutchinson, S. and Bromley, T. (2007) *The Challenges of Research Training Programmes* (Chapter 5 in *Skills Training in Research Degree Programmes: Politics and Practice*, Edited by Hinchcliffe, R., Bromley, T. and Hutchinson, S.) Open University Press.

Thiagarajan, S. (2006 25th Anniversary Edition) *Barnga: A Simulation Game on Cultural Clashes* Nicholas Brearley Publishing.

Additional Resources

While these references are not directly cited in the text, they are the books that we use when inspiration is in short supply. As such they set a lot of the tone for the types of activities herein.

Covey, S.A., Merrill, M. and Merrill, R.R. (1994) *First Things First* Simon and Schuster Ltd.

Epstein, R. (1996) *Creativity Games for Trainers* McGraw Hill.

Epstein, R. with Rogers, J. (2001) *The Big Book of Motivation Games* McGraw Hill.

Havergal, M. and Edmonstone, J. (2003) *The Facilitators Toolkit* Gower Publishing.

Kirwan, C. (2009) *Improving Learning Transfer* Gower Publishing.

Lambert, J. and Myers, S. (1994) *50 Activities for Diversity Training* HRD Press.

Martin, A., Franc, D. and Zounková, D. (2004) *Outdoor and Experiential Learning* Gower Publishing.

Newstrom, J. and Scannell, E. (1996) *The Big Book of Business Games* McGraw Hill.

Newstrom, J. and Scannell, E. (1998) *The Big Book of Team Building Games* McGraw Hill.

Orridge, M. (1996) *75 Ways to Liven Up Your Training: A Collection of Energizing Activities* Gower Publishing Ltd.

Pike, B. and Solem, L. (2000) *50 Creative Training Openers and Energisers* Pfeiffer.

Rodwell, J. (2007) *Activity-Based Training Design* Gower Publishing.

Scannell, E. and Newstrom, J. (1991) *Still More Games that Trainers Play* McGraw Hill.

Scannell, E. and Newstrom, J. (1994) *Even More Games that Trainers Play* McGraw Hill.

Solem, L. and Pike, B. (1997) *50 Creative Training Closers* Pfeiffer/John Wiley.

Tamblyn, D. and Weiss, S. (2000) *The Big Book Humorous Training Games* McGraw Hill.

Thiagarajan, S. and Parker, G. (1999) *Teamwork and Teamplay* Jossey Bass/Pfeiffer.

Whitworth, L., Kinsey-House, H. and Sandahl, P. (2007 2nd Edition) *Coactive Coaching* Davies-Black Publishing.

Woodcock, M. (1979) *Team Development Manual* Gower Publishing Ltd.

If you have found this book useful you may be interested in other titles from Gower

Pattern Making, Pattern Breaking:
Using Past Experience and New Behaviour
in Training, Education and Change Management
Ann Alder
Hardback: 978-0-566-08853-7
ebook: 978-1-4094-1911-2

The Facilitator's Toolkit
Maggie Havergal and John Edmonstone
Hardback: 978-0-566-08565-9
Looseleaf: 978-0-566-08493-5

The Large Group Facilitator's Manual:
A Collection of Tools for Understanding, Planning
and Running Large Group Events
Kerry Napuk and Eddie Palmer
Looseleaf: 978-0-566-08418-8

The Fast Facilitator:
76 Facilitator Activities and Interventions Covering Essential
Skills, Group Processes and Creative Techniques
Anthony Landale and Mica Douglas
Looseleaf: 978-0-566-08393-8

Games for Legendary Away Days
Karen Cooley and Kirsty McEwan
Hardback: 978-0-566-08606-9

Outdoor and Experiential Learning:
An Holistic and Creative Approach to Programme Design
Andy Martin, Dan Franc and Daniela Zounková
Hardback: 978-0-566-08628-1

Emotional Games for Training:
15 Games that Explore Feelings, Behaviour and Values
Ken Jones
Hardback: 978-0-566-08497-3

GOWER